Never Push When It Says Pull

NEVER PUSH WHEN IT SAYS PULL
SMALL RULES FOR LITTLE PROBLEMS

Guy Browning

ATLANTIC BOOKS
LONDON

First published in hardback in Great Britain in 2005
by Atlantic Books on behalf of Guardian Newspapers Ltd.
Atlantic Books is an imprint of Grove Atlantic Ltd.

9 8 7 6 5 4 3

A CIP record for this book is available from the British Library.

ISBN 1 84354 473 3

Printed and bound in Great Britain by
Mackays of Chatham plc, Chatham Kent
Design by Patty Rennie
Typeset by Avon DataSet Ltd, Bidford on Avon, Warwickshire

Guardian Books
Ormond House
26–27 Boswell Street
London
WC1N 3JZ

This book is dedicated with love to
my gorgeous wife Esther.

Many thanks to the creative hothouse that is Ross Woodford, David Belcher and David Christensen.

Also thanks to the publishing giants Kate Jones, Katharine Viner, Toby Mundy, Louisa Joyner, Alice Hunt, Karen Duffy and Lisa Darnell.

And finally, respect and admiration for the legendary Graeme Wilkinson.

Contents

Out and About

How to... use a lift

Calling a lift is easy. Simply press the button and wait. And then press the button again. Many lifts work on the pressure you exert on the call button, so hitting it a hundred times will make it arrive a lot faster. Before you get into the lift, it's as well to check whether it's going up or down. There's nothing more embarrassing than saying confidently to a packed lift 'Ground floor please' and then feeling the lift rocketing upwards.

Getting into a crowded lift is like entering a mini party. Everyone's already settled in there and when the doors open they all look at you as if to say, 'You're not coming in here.' Just take a big breath, step in and then say something to break the ice such as, 'You're probably wondering why I called you all here.'

This difficult entry moment explains why even when the lift is the size of your living room and there's only one small lady in it, the tendency is to wait for the next one. If the same lady is in the next one, it could be her job to operate the lift, so just get in and stop being so silly.

In a crowded lift it's very bad manners ever to face

anybody head on. You should always try and be at least 90 degrees to your neighbours so that an aerial view would look as if you were all finding your way around a particularly tight maze.

Never talk to someone in a lift unless you know which button they've pressed and you can tailor your conversation to the exact second. Restrict yourself to saying 'Morning'. In a lift it's acceptable to say this at any time of night or day, because you're in your own little world without daylight. The other word everyone wants to say in a lift, especially when the little bell pings, is 'lingerie'. Don't say this unless you're with people you know and love or you're absolutely positive the other person is getting out.

You're allowed to look at a stranger in a lift a maximum of once, then you must look elsewhere for the duration of your trip. That's why it's a relief when everyone gets out and leaves you alone in the lift. You're then free to pull faces in the mirror, say 'lingerie' loudly and pass wind extravagantly. Often at this moment you'll discover that the little lady is still in the lift with you.

Being in a lift means invading someone else's body space. This can be quite exciting when two people are attracted to each other. Passions often ignite in lifts and are sometimes even consummated. This can be awkward for the other passengers, even at 90 degrees.

How to... use a library

Libraries are brothels for the mind. Which means that librarians are the madams, greeting the punters, understanding their strange tastes and needs and then pimping their books. That's rubbish of course but it does wonders for the image of librarians.

Libraries were the original Internet. All knowledge was available even in your local branch library. You could order a book and if they didn't have it, they would get it from another library in Yorkshire that did. This would then give you the double pleasure of having the book you wanted and the knowledge that a Yorkshireman somewhere would be searching in vain for it. Of course many libraries now have free Internet access which is very useful for looking things up online such as the opening times for the library.

There are two types of books in libraries – Catherine Cooksons and non-Catherine Cooksons. The non-Catherine Cooksons are big books like *Britain's Railways from the Air* for men to browse through while their wives choose a Cookson.

When you're in a library it's important to respect the signs saying 'Silence'. It's common courtesy therefore to speak quietly when you're on your mobile phone. For those who find keeping silent very difficult there are special rooms where you can go and shout your head off. Look for the sign 'Local History Archives'.

Some remote rural areas have mobile libraries which drive around very slowly so that the books don't fall off the shelves. Often it can take half an hour to negotiate a roundabout without the Britannicas shifting. Because mobile libraries can't be everywhere, they are absolute sticklers for late books and will quite happily block your drive with their van until you hand back your *Tintin in Tibet.*

In most libraries there is a section of large-print books. The print is so large in these books that most of the text has to be removed. For example, in *One Hundred Years of Solitude* you'll be lucky to get *Forty Years of Moderate Loneliness*. What makes this even more of a swiz is that they only ever tell you about this in the small print.

Pensioners use libraries much the same way as junkies use dealers. An average pensioner will read an entire library in a year. Once they get hooked on a Barbara Taylor Bradford they will need that same high time and time again. Eventually they move on to something slightly harder like a Maeve Binchy or a Beryl Bainbridge. Finally, they end up stuck in a lonely room somewhere, mainlining bookclub offers. This is all rubbish, of course, but it does wonders for the image of librarians.

How to... queue

In the noble art of queuing Britain stands first, second and third amongst the nations of the world principally because the other nations of the world aren't really queuing up for that kind of recognition.

To join a queue you need to judge distance very accurately; allow the same amount of space as you would to dance with your Aunt Erica at a wedding. Beware of leaving too much space otherwise you'll become that horrible chink in the queue through which people pass. If you can touch the person in front of you with your tongue, you're too close.

When you're in a long queue you must all look in the same direction. It simply isn't done to face backwards as this is tantamount to an invasion of privacy. If people can't see the back of your head, they won't know you're in front of them. Let's face it, we would never have got off the beaches at Dunkirk if our lads had all been facing different directions.

Long queues inch forward and it's vital that you take every inch when presented. You can't wait until a couple of feet have opened up and then make a big leap forward because the person behind you will immediately ask, 'Are you in the queue?', by which they mean, 'Don't you even know how to queue properly?'. Queues edge forward even when the front isn't going anywhere. When you're in a queue it's advisable not to lean or tilt forward because the three hundred people behind you will all budge up into the vacant inches and you'll never get them back.

There is a hierarchy in queues. Being first in the queue is next to godliness. Being able to see the front of the queue is excellent. Being able to see people who can see the front is not bad. Seeing nothing but queue is not good and being at the very back of the queue is dreadful. The only thing that'll make you feel better is when some poor loser joins the queue behind you.

Some queues get a little bit messy and to the outsider it may not be immediately apparent who is in front. However, every single person in the queue has a mental photo-finish picture of exactly who is where. That's why queue jumpers are the lowest form of life as they offend our deep sense of fair play. People who lead crushingly oppressed lives will stand for just about any indignity but God forbid if anybody should push in a queue in front of them.

Queuing is a serious, skilled occupation and you'll notice that loving couples never claim to have met in a queue. Unless you've got a back of the neck to die for, you shouldn't expect to score there either.

How to... be polite

Being polite is a combination of saying please, thank you and letting other people do things before you do them. If at any time you slip up and accidentally do something you want to do or do it before someone else wants to do it, you must make up for this by sending a thank-you card immediately.

Passing tasty food items to others before you help yourself is a very good way of showing how polite you are and also of rapidly losing weight. Giving up your seat to a woman is frowned upon in these days of sexual equality, so if you really want to be polite to a woman why not give up your job instead.

Holding doors open is another minefield. Obviously if it's a swing door or revolving door, any attempt to hold it open is going to make you look like a complete tool. If you've held a door open for one person and the entire population of the UK seems to be following them through, eventually you'll have to let it go. This will inevitably coincide with the arrival of the pregnant lady vicar on crutches.

The underlying principle of politeness is putting the desires and wishes of others before your own. Where this goes terribly wrong is in the bedroom. There is no such thing as a polite erection. (Occasionally you have one you can open doors with but that's slightly different.)

Politeness used to revolve round the placing of doilies under everything. The verbal equivalent of a doily is to preface everything you say with 'I wonder' and to include the concept of 'not minding' in the sentence. Doing this means it's almost impossible to be rude; 'I wonder if you wouldn't mind not being such an arse' sounds positively friendly.

In life-threatening emergencies, politeness can be a mixed blessing. When you're trying to get out of a burning aircraft, holding the door open for others to escape is a good way of finishing yourself off. On the other hand, if you're on death row, giving your seat up to someone else has the opposite effect.

When two polite people meet nothing happens and you're just left with a pool of antimatter; no doors can be passed, chairs sat in, food eaten or initiatives taken – there is just a quivering of latent energy ready to be turned into thank-you cards. Really, really polite people may seem to be dull but they all have a little secret. Once you have the reputation for being polite you can get away with saying things like, 'My word, what an interesting story', to people who could bore a new Channel tunnel.

How to... embarrass yourself

You don't realize how important your dignity is until you suddenly lose it. Falling and breaking a hip is clearly a tragedy but tripping on a paving slab and doing that sudden monkey spasm trip walk thing is rich street comedy.

During your trip everyone within a mile radius will see you and laugh themselves sick inside. Immediately after your stumble, you will try to give the impression that a little tripping movement is a normal part of your walking pattern and hardly worth noticing. However, even when you've just had a little trip, you completely forget how to walk afterwards and it feels like you're doing some kind of stilted stagger. A mile or two later these feelings begin to wear off, and you resume walking normally, just in time for your other foot to hit another wonky paving slab.

Watching where you're putting your feet will reduce the chance of tripping in the street. At the same time it will increase the likelihood of banging your head on a piece of low scaffolding. People with their finger on the nuclear trigger are kept well clear of low beams and scaffolding because if they were to hit their head really hard, the world would be the first thing to get punished.

Embarrassing yourself doesn't have to be physical. Just getting someone's name wrong will do it. Especially if you call your boss mum, your teacher dad or your wife Brian. These are called Freudian slips. Freudian trips are even worse. This is where you slip on a banana skin just as you were thinking how much bananas resemble the sexual organ.

Oddly, it's the smallest things that embarrass people the most. No one minds being caught naked on camera during a live broadcast to the nation. But if you ask someone a question, pretend to be interested in the answer and then ask them the exact same question again seconds later, you might just as well walk into a corner and stay there. Another top clanger is to ask someone how their friend/relative is when you've forgotten that they're in fact dead. Saying 'Still dead?' won't help.

Having your flies undone is supposed to be embarrassing but isn't. In fact men don't mind it at all as it implies that there's rather a lot of activity in that neck of the woods. For women, tucking their skirt into their knickers is conceptually embarrassing but as they can never actually see the damage, it doesn't seem quite real. For women in this knickers-in-skirt state, it's more embarrassing when they're closely followed by a man with his flies undone.

In any acutely uncomfortable situation, the quickest way out of it is to bang your head on something low and hard as this trumps any other concurrent embarrassment.

How to… be a model citizen

Model citizens forward mail to the previous occupants of their house for seventeen years after they've moved. They do their income tax return on the afternoon of April the 5th to catch the first post on the 6th. And they fill it in with black ink and clear capitals. They also declare income found down the back of the sofa.

Model citizens don't drop rubbish. They actually pick up rubbish and put it into bins. If there are no bins they will take eight crushed beer cans home in their handbag, despite thc risk of being identified as a closet alcoholic. Model citizens volunteer for things. They are on the board of governors of the local school even when they don't have children. They shake charity tins for twelve straight hours which is the exercise equivalent of clean and jerking three tons.

Model citizens can't see a policeman without putting the kettle on. In the Neighbourhood Watch, model citizens catalogue every movement of everything so that crimes can be re-enacted in more detail than they were actually committed. Model citizens keep off grass of all descriptions. The idea of them walking across a restricted municipal lawn is as unlikely as them lighting a seven-inch spliff in Waitrose.

In municipal swimming baths model citizens don't run, canoodle, bomb or leave plasters on the side of the pool. They also have a shower before entering the baths. They swim in lanes even if there aren't any. They also keep a weather eye out for children suffering from negative buoyancy.

When travelling by train, model citizens have their ticket ready for inspection at all times. They also like to lightly eavesdrop in case they can be of any assistance with timetable enquiries. On alighting from the train, the model citizen will have remembered, checked and counted all his belongings and taken them with him. He will also close as many train doors as need closing to expedite the train's departure. It's perhaps fortunate that model citizens don't generally carry a whistle, otherwise they'd be sending the train on its way.

The airborne model citizen will keep his seatbelt loosely fastened even when he's moving up and down the aisle. He'll also know the exact location of all emergency exits, bearing in mind that the nearest exit might be behind him. In the unlikely event of a landing on water, the model citizen will be the only one removing their high-heeled shoes before using the slide.

Model citizens obey the letter of the Highway Code

although this is often because they drive cars mechanically unable to break the Highway Code. On a bicycle the model citizen does arm signals with his arms perpendicular to his body even if it means having to punch a hole in the side of a passing lorry. They also know how to signal right with their left hand. Sadly this is recognized by only 0.1 per cent of the population and regarded as a grave insult by the other 99.9 per cent.

How to... do jury service

Jury service is a government-sponsored project for people without access to television to experience the excitement and interest of courtroom dramas. When you are called up for jury service you have to attend unless you can prove you are doing vital work. Amazingly few people find their work is so vital that they can't immediately take a couple of weeks' paid holiday.

The most important part of jury service is the claim for expenses. This is enshrined in the Magna Carta and is the inalienable right of every freeborn Briton. The experience of being off work and actually claiming 'loss of earnings' is possibly the most satisfying part of the whole criminal justice system.

Once you arrive at the court there's a wait before you can start sweeping the criminal filth off our streets. First of all you have to be picked for a case from the pool of available jurors, many of whom appear to be exactly the sort of criminal filth of which the streets need cleaning.

Eventually, you get picked for a case and you file into the courtroom. Try not to whoop with excitement as this is not the desired tone. The first person you'll notice is the shifty, feckless, long-haired degenerate in the dock. This is the judge. It's the smart looking person in the suit and tie who's the criminal. (Barristers often call witnesses also in suits and ties. You are not allowed to find these people guilty even though some of them are crying out for it.)

At this stage you may feel the urge to find the criminal guilty but you should wait to hear what he's done before you bang him up for fifteen big ones. Sadly you're unlikely to find out because you'll have two of the finest minds in the country telling outrageous porkies. These are the barristers. Their job is to confuse everyone and everything but in a very impressive, masterful way.

The good thing about the jury 'retiring' is that there are no barristers in the jury room. Juries often spend a long time deliberating principally because they have to try and salvage the truth from in amongst all the barristers' whoppers.

Once you get into the jury room, everyone argues for ten hours about whether they can smoke or not. Then people divide into the reasonable doubters (he could have had that assault knife for whittling craft objects) and the no smoke without firers (what was he doing there in the first place). Eventually, when the pressure for a cigarette is too intense you reach a verdict.

On your way home you wonder about two things: whether he really was guilty and why you're being followed by a mob of angry relatives carrying assault knives. If you've really come up with a bizarre verdict, you may find a barrister following you with an assault knife.

How to... do amateur dramatics

There are two kinds of amateur dramatics. One is the unwilling career path of soap stars who leave their soaps to avoid typecasting and never work again. The other is what people who want to be soap stars do after they've finished working all day at the carpet shop.

Saying you do amateur dramatics is the quickest possible way of ruling yourself out of consideration at any professional casting. You may have done the finest Lear in the living memory of the Scout hut but it puts you five rungs below the third spear-carrier at the National Theatre.

People do amateur dramatics for many reasons but primarily because there isn't a witchcraft and satanic rites circle in their area. Amateur dramatics is a great excuse for meeting new people, dressing up and then sneaking off behind the scenery and getting undressed together.

In all amateur dramatics societies you have a very similar cast. Firstly there is the president of the society who has a beard, is in early retirement and always casts himself as lead male whether that's Hamlet or John Travolta in Grease. He has a deep, rich voice which he perfects through continual use. There is a lady of similar age who, in the worst-case scenario, is the wife of Hamlet/Travolta. She generally can't act for toffee and gets to prove it at great length with the biggest female part.

Best entertainment value in any play is the young man with the acting talent of an ironing board. He's wooden in his normal life and he brings this experience to any part he plays. He is always word-perfect often because he's only given ten of them in total. In dramatic tension terms his appearance on stage is equivalent to a local anaesthetic.

No cast is complete without the resident comedian. He can recite Monty Python sketches verbatim and ad nauseam. He also has his own collection of funny walks, voices and facial hair. Look out for his party piece Victor Meldrew impression, especially during a particularly dark and tragic part of the play.

In every group there is one passably attractive young woman who believes she is on the high road to the Hollywood A-list. The bearded president can generally help her get there if only she'd do more private rehearsals with him. Of the entire production the most talented and gifted performer is almost always the prompt. He has to be because he says about 50 per cent of the entire lines of the play in all the different characters.

Amateur dramatics societies generally do one production a year. That's how long it takes for the various divorces, remarriages and pregnancies from the last one to have subsided.

How to... fundraise

There are two types of informal economy in this country: one is the black economy where people work for cash in hand; the other is the fundraising economy where people work for cash in tin. It's estimated that at any given time the British public are trying to raise more for good causes than the entire economy of Belgium (please give generously).

Jumble sales are the bedrock of British fundraising. What happens is you clear out all your old junk and then buy some new junk to put in its place. In small communities some jumble has been circulating for five generations. When this happens, the jumble sale eventually graduates to an Antique Fayre.

Of all the ways of making money by far the most efficient is the cake stall. The coffee and walnut cake is well known to be the fastest money-making device since privatization of the major utilities. All funds could very quickly be raised purely by cake stalls were it not for the shortage of people who can actually make cakes.

For as long as there have been funds to raise, there

have been tombolas. This involves a table full of various prizes all with a raffle ticket taped to them. You buy a ticket and if you're very lucky you don't win anything. The 'winning' ticket is often a bottle of 'wine' that has survived six dinner parties untouched.

Many people fundraise through doing a sponsored activity. Sponsorship is a tax on friendship. It's a means by which you have to pay for your friend doing something foolish. The hardest part of any sponsored activity is getting the sponsorship in the first place. It's a wonder there isn't sponsored sponsorship raising. If you're getting sponsorship, always ask your most generous friend first so that they put £20 at the top of the sheet, rendering it almost impossible for people to put 25p underneath.

Shaking a tin in a public place is a great way of seeing what it's like to be totally invisible. Remember to put a few coppers in your tin before you start otherwise not only will no one see you, they won't hear you either. On the other hand, shouting for donations is a mistake, as this provides an early warning system for people to avoid you. If you really have to shout something, shout 'Cake!'.

To be fair there are some extremely generous people out there who will give to anything on the basis that if you're making the effort to collect, they should make the effort to give. You could therefore shake a tin marked 'Cigarettes and Loose Women for Me' and still make a healthy return.

How to... say goodbye

They say that goodbyes are mini-deaths. In fact they're more like mini-births, with a long struggle to separate yourself and get some fresh air.

Saying goodbye on the telephone is particularly tricky because you can't use any of the subtle body language signals like walking away. Instead there's an elaborate goodbye ritual that can start up to five minutes before the call ends. The first signal is to say that it has been nice talking to them implying that it's about to finish. Be very careful not to use the present tense and say, 'It's nice talking to you', as they'll take this as a green light to do yet more talking. Similarly, saying, 'I've got to go', isn't half as useful as, 'I'm going now', followed by the phone being put down.

Some people on the phone are like broadband, in that they're always on. You can put the phone down and lift it up several times in the conversation and they'll still be talking. Don't feel guilty about just ringing off abruptly, because they'll just continue talking to their spouse, fish or thin air.

Young people often think saying goodbye at a railway station will be romantic. When you arrive at the station you'll probably be at your peak of tearfulness and will have said all the high cheese things like, 'You know I'll wait for you.' Then you find that the train is an hour late and you suddenly decide that although you don't mind promising to wait for them, you'd really rather not wait with them, especially as the café's closed.

Even if the train's on time, the actual parting can be tricky. In modern trains you can't hang out of the window snogging because you can't get the windows open. Instead you have to stand on the platform mouthing silent rubbish through the double-glazed window. Then, just as the train moves out, someone fantastically attractive sits down opposite your beloved and smiles winningly at them.

Saying goodbye is only one part of the fiendishly complex process of taking one's leave. When you actually leave someone's presence you have to judge whether and when to look back and wave. Walking away without looking back can imply that you've forgotten all about someone. To be sure to avoid offence, wave till someone is out of sight. This may backfire if you can't see very well. You think they've gone but they've only taken a small step backwards. When this happens, you'll probably regret that you immediately said 'Good riddance.'

Never say one last parting remark. Nine times out of

ten the person leaving won't hear it. They then have to smile and laugh and pretend they heard you shouting, 'That's the wrong train.' Or they have to come all the way back and before you know it, you're saying hello again.

Home and Hearth

How to… fold things

As the world becomes increasingly crowded, so folding will become ever more important because folding things helps you fit more stuff into less space. Research has shown that 90 per cent of women who complain about lack of storage space for their clothing are strangers to folding. Most of us are already pretty familiar with folding thanks to the folding stuff. Only rich men in big coats with wallets like wine menus don't fold their cash.

Folding sheets used to be a big thing in the quaint old days when people used to wash their sheets. One person stood at each end of the sheet and both folded several times in completely different directions until one person got fed up and left. Then the other person had to fold it by standing on top of the wardrobe to get enough height to let the sheet hang straight before flicking it up and attempting to catch it halfway in a little fold. This performance explains why most people now use a duvet.

Things that fold out rather than in are huge fun because they suddenly go from two dimensions to three.

For example, fold-out chairs make you more aware of the joy of sitting and a fold-away bed helps you sleep better because you know that the alternative would be to sleep standing up. Fold-up furniture also has a built-in slapstick factor in that it's more than likely to fold up with you still in it. This slapstick factor is not always a good thing as you would, for example, hesitate before doing serious business with somebody who used a folding bicycle on a regular basis and who wasn't in the circus industry.

Folding things does three things: it makes things smaller, it makes them squarer and it gives you nice edges. That's why you can't get folding blancmange. Folding is about control and order and discipline. It can also be an incredibly frustrating and boring thing to do; too much of it and you end up wanting to cause havoc and mayhem. That's why army basic training consists of hours of folding and creasing things followed by bayonet practice.

Folding is an art and if you've ever seen someone try to fold a large newspaper in a crowded train you'll know that very few people have it. If you think you can fold things, try opening out an Ordnance Survey map and then folding it back so that all the creases go the same way. Research has shown that the likelihood of folding a map back the same way you unfolded it is significantly less than being hit by a block of frozen urine jettisoned from a passing airliner.

How to... iron

Since the fifties Britain has seen a steady decrease in creases. However, creases have never entirely gone because a small proportion of the population can't say what they want to say about themselves in a drip-dry non-iron synthetic bag.

Irons have three settings – two for women who wear delicates and one red-hot one for men who wouldn't be seen dead in a delicate of any description. Men can't conceive of having any tool on less than full power which is why, if men ever get hold of them, delicates look as if they've had a once-over with a blow torch and soldering iron. Generally though, men are quite sensible about ironing: if they really want something to look sharp and neat, they buy it that way and then wear it straight from the wrapping.

Mothers know that boys have a problem with ironing and have therefore evolved a cunning trick to get them started. They wait until boys are old enough to want to look grungy and then start ironing razor-sharp creases in all their trendy gear. Naturally, boys don't want to go out looking like a Victorian sailor on shore leave so they have to spend half an hour ironing out the creases and returning the trousers to the desired laundry basket state.

Work shirts take about fifteen minutes to iron as the manufacturers have contrived to put every ironing challenge into one item of clothing: collars, double cuffs, ruff sleeves, flared yokes, etc. Unless you like to spend your weekends at the ironing board, the best way to cope with this is to just iron the front of your shirt and keep your jacket on all day.

Pants don't need ironing. If you've reached the stage where a stranger is seeing your underpants then the necessity of impressing them with creased pants is probably past. In fact the last thing you want is to be almost finished ripping each other's clothes off and then for everything to come to a grinding halt while you try to explain away the neat little creases in your y-fronts.

Some items claim to be easy-iron but this can't be right as anything that involves grappling with an ironing board can't be easy. In the competition to design the deckchair, the losing team went on to design the ironing board. For a quick insight into the world of slapstick comedy simply try erecting an ironing board with one hand with a red-hot iron in the other (this is actually dangerous so don't try it at home).

Bizarre as it sounds, some people love ironing. It really all depends on what kind of person you are. Some people look rumpled even when they are wearing a starched bib and tucker whilst others manage to look sharply creased in the nude. The general rule is the more you look like an ironing board the more you enjoy their company.

How to... wash up

The world is divided into those people who do the washing up straight after dinner and those filthy degenerates who leave it to develop all kinds of killer spores overnight. Some people are so keen to get on with the washing up that you've barely got the last spoonful of pineapple jelly in your mouth before they're clattering away in the kitchen.

Dishwashers have made kitchens washing-up-free zones in the same way that computers have given us paperless offices i.e. they haven't. That's because dishwashers, even though they use enough water to supply a small trout farm, can still only manage to clean a flat plate with a few loosely attached crumbs.

In the days before sexual equality, men could demonstrate their commitment to female empowerment by washing up after Sunday lunch. They would tuck into the washing up blissfully unaware that most of the really nasty stuff had already been washed up well before luncheon was served.

Men washing up always complain about their tools. A

cloth is never enough: they need wire wool, some kind of stiff brush and industrial strength detergents. Men generally do about half the washing up and then they decide to 'leave the rest to soak'. Unchecked, these items would then be left to soak until the end of the football season.

The order in which you wash up is key: starting with a roasting tin and then going onto the sherry glasses is fine only if you're happy to have the world's greasiest sherry glasses for the vicar to juggle with next time he's round. Start with the sherry glasses and then go onto the heavy stuff. Then you can smash up all the sherry glasses with your casserole dish on the draining board.

To avoid this you need to do a little pre-wash-up of the sherry glasses and then immediately dry them with a freshly minted tea towel. This gets them out of the way and also prevents them smearing (if there's one thing vicars won't forgive you for, it's a smeary sherry glass).

Halfway through washing up, the water begins to resemble the Ganges during cremation high season. Only press on if all you've got left to do are Gran's old saucepans. Anything else is likely to come out dirtier than it went in. When you've finished, wipe down the surfaces and then pour the water away. Then refill the bowl for that one crucial item of glassware you invariably miss. Finally, remember that the washing up is not finished until the kettle is on for tea and more cup dirtying.

How to... do the washing

The washing machine is the continuously beating heart of the modern home. It's fed by the laundry basket and in turn feeds the airing cupboard. Actually wearing clothes is the shortest link in the washing cycle.

The wash can be divided into three parts: whites, darks and coloureds. Coloureds are what you get when you accidentally put one dark in with the whites. There are also things called delicates. Men don't recognize the existence of this group in the wash. Which is why women don't recognize their delicates after men have done the wash. Some items of clothing require hand washing. These items live at the bottom of the laundry basket and never come out. As a nation Britain withdrew from hand washing at roughly the same time and speed as it withdrew from the Empire.

Whatever the detergent manufacturers say, whites need to be done at 90 degrees. That's because whites generally include men's pants which are the ultimate washing challenge. In an ideal world, men's underpants should be taken out into the backyard and shot. This isn't a cost effective option so they have to be boiled several times to get them back to some sort of decency.

Soap now comes in powder, tablet, gel or liquid form which can then go in the drawer, the wash, the bag or the ball. They all wash whiter than white which actually means off-white. Similarly they all make your wash smell great. Just press the washing to your nose and breathe in the summer flowers. But don't try this with men's underpants even after seven consecutive washings.

You can dry your clothes in a dryer but this leads to a lot of static electricity. Pulling your nightie on after tumble drying is like being in the middle of an electrical storm and leaves you with a Ken Dodd hairstyle. Drying on the line outside is best unless you live in Manchester where you actually do the pre-soaking on the line outside. Urban people dry their clothes by draping them over things. That's why you'll notice that the T-shirt of your grungy urban male often has the residual shape of a banister or radiator still in it.

Alternatively you can use drying racks. These take fourteen hours to load up and getting your smalls on the bottom rungs is equivalent to some of the black belt positions in yoga. You can clear the same rack in fourteen seconds between the first and second ring of your sophisticated new girlfriend at the door.

In every house there is a sock orphanage where sad little unloved socks live until their partner can be found.

Often their partner is never found. That's because the washing machine demands a ritual sacrifice of one sock per wash to placate its inner workings.

How to... keep tidy

Everything in life has its proper place. If it's not in that place it is officially untidy. If the thing doesn't have a proper place in the first place then it is officially rubbish.

Remember that one person's tidiness is another person's chaos. Often these two people live together. There are three levels of untidiness: the first is towels on floor; the second is towels stuffed on towel rail; the final level is towel hung neatly over the rail with no discernible wrinkles.

The acid test of whether you are naturally untidy is if you answer yes to the following questions: does your car currently have any food or drink packaging on the floor; do you feel that straightening a duvet once you're up is completely unnecessary; are your CDs divorced from their cases for years at a time?

Few roles are reserved for modern man but taking out the bins is one. It's like hunter-gathering in reverse. Bins are vital for tidy people but are a constant source of irritation because they're full of rubbish. Some super-tidy people eventually decide that even the bin is cluttering up the place and it gets thrown out in a kind of existential implosion.

A wastepaper basket is too large if it takes more than a month to fill. Anything over a month and there's a real danger of it becoming a compost. A correctly sized bin should be able to fit comfortably over your head but not when you're wearing a cycling helmet.

Some people's houses are so neat and tidy that there at first appears to be no sign of life. It's often very difficult to go to the lavatory in these houses, partly because your bowels are too afraid to move but more importantly because there will inevitably be a freak accident where you end up peeing up the walls and all over the curtains.

The secret to tidiness is storage space; some people put things away in cupboards, other people view entire rooms as large cupboards, in that as long as things are in a room and the door is closed, everything in it is tidy.

Young children are also obsessed with tidying but in a negative way in that they spend a lot of time untidying. It's their way of showing that they can change the universe around them. Tidying in later life is an attempt to put the universe back where it was. In general it's worth remembering that life is a messy, chaotic business but underneath there is a clearly discernible pattern. It just takes a lifetime of tidying before you can see it.

How to... assemble furniture

Every weekend millions of people attempt to build a piece of furniture. It is the modern equivalent of riding into the Valley of Death.

Many people mistakenly assume that furniture you build yourself comes in a pack smaller than the finished item. In fact the reverse is true. An average size bedside cabinet will fold down into a flat pack the size of a squash court.

You then have to get this colossal flat pack home. You can save time and your marriage by accepting from the word go that there is no angle that it will fit inside your car without you having to lie flat on the seat and drive home in reverse.

The golden rule once you've got it home is never try and construct the furniture by yourself or with anyone else. For men especially, being able to single-handedly construct a piece of furniture is a clear test of masculinity right up there with parallel parking, throwing a ball and getting served at a bar. If you're a woman and tired of your current relationship, simply pop your head round the door and say, 'Shouldn't that bit go there?'.

Fortunately, most flat packs come with clear instructions in seventeen languages. Unfortunately none of them will be English. If you look hard enough, one set of instructions might be in English but not as we know it. For example, a critical instruction might read, 'Conform the plane before bedwet.' The only way round this is to look at the pictures really, really carefully, especially the one featuring the bit you don't have.

Thorough people who think flat pack furniture erection is simply a matter of being careful and systematic will often lay out the pieces before they start. This is when they find that two security screw twisters are missing. There is a way of finding these two pieces and that is to make the whole thing without having counted the pieces in the first place and then you will find you have them left at the end.

You would have thought that a bookshelf wouldn't have too many opportunities for construction error. If you thought that, you thought wrong. There are seventeen billion different ways you can put those nine pieces together. During construction you often get a sneaky suspicion that something is not right. At this point most men simply press on, applying superhuman force and an increasing range of power tools from the shed. And if the vanity unit ends up as kitchen trolley, so be it.

Finally, your piece of furniture is complete. This will give you a lifetime of pleasure as long as you make sure that you don't put any books in the case, clothes in the wardrobe or paper on the desk.

How to... change the duvet cover

Whenever you get the feeling that mankind is at the top of the evolutionary tree and that our civilization is a great and wonderful thing, see if you can change a duvet cover without looking like a complete idiot.

Changing the duvet cover is nature's way of punishing you for not making the bed for the last six months. Sports scientists have shown that changing a duvet cover is the equivalent of an intermediate course of yoga and a four-mile run. Mentally, the whole process is the equivalent of attempting to parallel park in three dimensions. If your duvet isn't a square one, then it's like parallel parking while being strapped upside down in your car.

You would have thought that putting a cover on would be as simple as putting a square peg into a square hole. Unfortunately something odd happens so that as soon as the duvet comes into contact with the cover it loses all its corners. Once you've finally got hold of one corner you can pass the entire duvet through your hands and never find another.

The chimneysweep method is where you take two small children, give them a corner of the duvet each and send them into the cover. View their progress from the outside and then turn their favourite video on when they have reached the corners. Button up the duvet cover, and then shake it down, checking that there are no remaining children inside.

The condom method is where you make sure the cover is rolled up and the duvet is fully stretched out. Then roll the cover down the outside of the duvet and button up at the bottom. This method, practised every night, is itself an effective method of contraception.

The spinnaker method is very effective especially for tall people. Firstly, pull the duvet cover over your head and stretch it out like a big sail. Then walk carefully around the room until you have located your duvet. Without letting go of the cover corners, bend down and pick up the duvet with your teeth. Stand up pulling the duvet up with you. Once standing up, use one arm at a time to locate a duvet corner and pull it into the corner of the cover. Finally, fall face forward onto the bed and wriggle out of the cover, leaving the duvet inside.

Men have come up with a novel and ingenious way of solving the duvet changing problem. They leave it on until a thick layer of sweat welds it permanently to the duvet. When things get really bad, they move house.

How to… live cleanly

The golden rule of healthy living is to make sure you keep your total units of alcohol below your total number of cigarettes. If you take your total units of alcohol, divide by the number of cigarettes and then add five points for every use of drugs in a week, you'll have clear proof that none of these things impairs your ability to do complicated mental arithmetic.

People who drink and smoke often like to boast that they're a sixty fags a day woman or fourteen pints a night man. Clean-living people have five portions of vegetables a day, so why not give up the booze and fags and instead become a ten portions of veg a day man. This sounds equally impressive.

One of the good things about smoking is that it gives you something to do with your hands. Try ditching the cigarettes and using your hands so intensively to describe everything that people mistake you for someone from the continent. Fiddling with the pack is also an essential part of the theatre of smoking. When you want a cigarette, spend half an hour fiddling with the pack, then put the cigarette behind your ear to 'save for later'. A good sized ear can store up to seven cigarettes in this way.

The definition of clean living is when you feel better getting out of bed than you did getting in. Unclean living is where you feel great going to bed but dreadful in the morning. Remember, you should never smoke in bed but, if you do, make sure you have a few pints at the same time because it's much harder to set fire to a wet bed.

Instead of nicotine and alcohol, there are many natural highs to enjoy all around us: church bells, thrushes, the wind in the trees. But you should exercise moderation even when it comes to natural highs. If you find you're becoming a twenty thrushes a day man, you might want to have a cigarette instead.

Smoking helps you concentrate. At work, regular smokers can concentrate intensely through long meetings keeping their mind focused on one thing, generally on how soon they can have another cigarette. If cigarettes help you to think, then drink helps you stop thinking. Clean living steers a middle way between thinking and not thinking by thinking pure thoughts. Sadly, pure thoughts are like rice cakes in that however many you have, you still feel you're missing something.

People who live uncleanly have a very distinctive smell, very similar to a pub's carpet. Clean-living people smell of a combination of Sea Breezes, Pine and Citrus Zest. In fact just sniffing a clean-living person is the equivalent of one portion of vegetables.

How to… clean your house

Cleaning is the penalty we pay for not living naked in the wilds. When you don't wash your hair, it starts to clean itself after a few weeks. When you don't clean your house for a few weeks, it looks like Tutankhamun's tomb.

One of the awful things about cleaning is that you can't start it until you've done tidying. And you can't do tidying until you've done sorting and you can't do that until you've got fundamental problems in your relationship ironed out or watched the football.

Men should be obliged by law to clean toilet bowls. Unbeknown to women, men never lift the seat ever. Lifting the seat would create a larger target area and less of a challenge. In fact sometimes we bounce up and down and shake things around just to make life more difficult for ourselves. Naturally this sometimes causes accidents but they're difficult to spot in the dark.

Men don't clean very often but when they do they like to hoover. The Hoover has an engine therefore it must be a toy. Men like to see just how much a Hoover can suck up and will happily spend a couple of hours sucking the crumbs from the toaster, the curtains from the wall and the topsoil from the garden.

Dust is the silent particulate presence of your mother-in-law in the house. Seeing dust anywhere gives you the sickening feeling that her finger will find it on her regular flying inspections. Dust, like poison, can be removed by sucking. Modern vacuum cleaners allow you to pick up all the dust from various rooms and then transfer it to your lungs, hair and clothing as you try to change the bag, bin, filter, etc.

Lime scale is the waterborne equivalent of dust. Catalogues often show models in the shower delicately arranged to cover their naughty bits. If they were simply to have a quick shower in a hard-water area they would be virtually invisible because there would be more limestone in the shower than in the entire Peak District.

Cleaning solutions come in two flavours, lemon or pine. Never use the two together unless you want to end up with a funny tropical pine forest smell. Really effective cleaning solutions remove fingerprints from all surfaces including your fingers.

Cleaners are divided into those who clean behind the fridge and those who sweep loose frozen peas under the fridge. Some people clean religiously to purge their inner demons and some people clean because they've lost a member of the family under the rubble. Some people use rubber gloves to clean the house. This is slightly eccentric because you didn't use protective equipment to make the house filthy so why use it to clean the place up.

It's a great feeling when the cleaning is over and you can relax in a sparkling house. This is the moment you decide that if things got bad you could clean houses for a living. Or you decide that things have got bad and you're going to get a cleaner. Attitudes to cleaning have changed now and many people have a cleaner. This is still only acceptable for domestic cleaning – people would be a little bit surprised if you had a weekly cleaner in to tackle your armpits.

How to… open stiff lids

For some people life is all jam, for others it's just a jar with a stiff lid. Once you've got a stiff lid, the first thing to do is to get a wet dishcloth. This gives you a better grip on the lid but the downside is that it can give you a smelly hand.

Feminists will do anything rather than hand the jam to a man as this would be a pathetic act of submission. What they may have overlooked is the terror in a man's heart when the jam is passed their way. The stiff lid rite of passage is one few men relish. That's why men often like to get tools involved at this point. There are special mole grips that can grip anything. However, there's something about getting your toolbox out that takes the edge off a relaxing breakfast.

The best way forward is to stop and mentally dominate the lid. You get yourself into a frame of mind that even if the lid were welded shut it would now glide off. Generally this technique works well. Even if it doesn't, you end up so mentally energized you can often go without breakfast.

Try running the lid under a hot tap. The water should be absolutely scalding. You then grab the lid, burn your hand and the sheer pain and anger will allow you to rip the top of the lid off without even bothering with the unscrewing action.

Jams are vacuum packed and it is atmospheric pressure that holds the lid firm. Observing the fundamental laws of physics, it stands to reason that the higher you go the less the pressure will be and the more easily you will open the jam jar. Going upstairs with the jam should therefore significantly reduce the pressure. And take the rest of breakfast upstairs to your partner while you're at it.

You can sometimes break the seal by giving the jar a sharp knock on the edge of a table. The top of the lid will suddenly go ping and you'll know resistance is over. Alternatively there will be a sudden crash and you'll know that you've got glass on toast for breakfast.

Another way of breaking the vacuum is to pierce a hole in the lid. Remember that at any given time one third of people in A&E have attempted to do this. Jam jar piercing is the most common knife wound in Britain.

The ultimate weapon you have in the war against stiff lids is to wedge the lid between the door and door frame. This will give you a vice-like grip on the lid. Of course this implies that you can get the door open and that it isn't itself stuck. Or, God forbid, jammed.

Reading and Writing

How to... write a novel

Rule number one is don't have a short, bald hero who isn't very interesting – if you start with him you're just making a rod for your own back.

Before you start you need to decide how fat your book is going to be. If it's going to be a doorstop, you'll have to fill a lot of pages by describing things in great detail as if people had never seen, for example, a house. Or you can introduce a vast army of minor characters who are briefly amusing but then suddenly get killed or emigrate to Canada.

The longer the book, the shorter the title: one word titles for over six hundred pages, e.g. *Quagmire*, one syllable titles for over one thousand pages, e.g. *Quag*. Very short books must have long titles such as *Yesterdays of Ephemera*. You can get away with titles like this because once you've read the title you've picked up most of the plot and are a good way through the text. Short books have sad endings because in order to have a happy ending you have to start happy, get sad and then regain happiness. Short books don't have time for all this, so they start miserable and get worse quickly.

Fashion applies to novels as it does to everything else. These days publishers won't be breaking your door down to sign up *Tea with Mr Piffin* or *Let's Put a Stopper on the Hun*. Seamy undersides are all the rage especially if the overside of your underside isn't very pleasant either. The general rule is that books are miserable. Only one book a century gets away with the bright underside of the lovely overside. If life was that cheery, people wouldn't be reading books, they'd be outside frolicking.

They say you should write about what you know. Whoever they are, they're talking rubbish. This is a trick by publishers to stop stamp collectors getting their novels published even though they've got snappy one-word titles like *Unhinged*. The great thing about fiction is that you can make it all up without doing a jot of research about anything. As long as you have one gratuitous fact per page, readers will think you know about nuclear fission/Iceland/micro-surgery.

All novels these days must have long passages of gratuitous sex. These are very difficult to write if you've never had any gratuitous sex, let alone long passages of it. If you make it up, there's always the danger that you'll make some fundamental biological error that will embarrass you in print for ever. This is possibly the only time when it's an advantage to have a short bald hero with the sexual magnetism of a face flannel.

How to… read books

Books are little hand-held parallel universes. Someone reading a book is likely to be living a far more exciting life on the page than in reality. Interestingly, one of the things you don't find characters in books doing is sitting down and reading a book for a couple of hours. Especially in thrillers.

Research has shown that any book over an inch thick is read fifteen times less than one under an inch thick. Readers have an instinctive cut-off point where they simply don't believe that any story could be that long, or any character that interesting.

Hardback buyers are superior to paperback buyers in every way especially in the muscles required to keep half a hundredweight of paper aloft. Never read a large hard-back in the bath if your feet don't rest comfortably on the far end. By the end of chapter two you'll be underwater.

Not all books are bought new. Antique books are bought by people who collect rather than read while second-hand books are bought by people who read rather than collect. A used paperback will often have little notes scribbled in the margins. This is done by the same people who talk to themselves loudly in public. Reading their old books is like being trapped in a parallel universe with a madman.

Apparently there is a skill that people pay to acquire called speed reading. This makes as much sense as taking a course in speed lovemaking. If you told an author you'd sped read their book they'd quite justifiably feel short changed. Similarly, you wouldn't like it if they'd speed written it.

When you're reading at normal speed, it's nice to pause at the end of a chapter. The maximum number of pages people will read to get to the end of a chapter is five. Important serious authors sometimes forget to have chapters altogether and you then have to mark your place in the book. Nice people mark their books with a book mark. When you don't finish a book, the book mark serves as a permanent reminder of where you lost interest (and also your incredibly poor taste in book marks). Folding the top corners of the page over is like marking your territory by peeing on it. You know where you've been but no one else will ever want to go there.

Occasionally you'll find a book where the pages have been marked by the blood of a husband who doesn't want to read in bed and insists on putting the light out to sleep. This is a bit harsh because dreams are just badly edited fiction for speed readers.

How to... sing

Singing is what you do when you want to make a noise but haven't got anything much to say. A lot of animals, birds and wildlife also sing. Whale song is a particularly good effort especially when you consider they're doing it underwater.

Just because you can't sing doesn't mean you can't sing. There's just as much fun to be had belting out 'I Will Survive' with every note completely wrong because, if you can't sing the right notes, it's unlikely that you'll hear the right notes. Others will of course notice and You May Not Survive. If challenged you can always say it's the jazz version because there are two things you can't argue with in life, jazz and hedges.

The favourite place for people who don't normally sing to sing is in the bath because everyone sounds like Pavarotti in there, no one can throw things at you in the bath, and the shower-head makes a perfect microphone. One has to wonder what Pavarotti would sound like in the bath, although one perhaps should also wonder whether the bath has yet been built that could accommodate Pavarotti.

When you've grown up singing hymns at school, you often find yourself singing hymns when peeling potatoes or doing other mundane things. As you can generally only remember the first two lines of every hymn, you have to make the rest of them up and for some reason the lyrics always get more and more obscene until you are singing absolute filth at the top of your voice.

People always feel safe singing at home because they think they are in a world of their own. You are in fact surrounded by neighbours who can hear every note. The only reason they don't complain is because they previously lived under the flight path of Heathrow and they developed a certain resistance to that kind of noise.

Karaoke is all the rage because it gives you all you need to sing properly but without the bath. The only drawback is that you have to sing in front of everyone from the office which makes you feel more naked than when you're actually in the bath. Church services are also a form of karaoke in that you are given the lyrics and then have to sing along to a backing track from Mrs Witherspoon on the organ. The only difference is that you aren't supposed to be completely cabbaged before singing in church.

In the old days there were folk songs that everyone could sing like 'There Was an Old Man Called Michael Finnigan'. With these songs you could start singing and everyone would join in with the next line. The youth of today are brought up on 'Smack My Bitch Up'. You could try and start singing it but no one's going to join in bccause it doesn't have a second line. Or if someone else starts singing it, simply hijack the song by adding, 'She had whiskers on her chinnigan'.

How to... be scientific

Science is the religion for people who can't cope with religion. The core belief is that science is an objective way of accessing the truth. Naturally there are as many scientific truths as there are scientists because God (or science) hasn't yet built an objective human being. Scientific facts and theories come and go like catwalk fashions and as with fashions you are completely beyond the pale in the scientific community if you don't immediately start wearing them.

Like most religions, science has its particular way of doing things which is called scientific method. This is where you have an idea and conduct experiments to see whether the idea stands up. There are as many experiments as there are ideas, so sooner or later you will match up your idea with the right experiment and the idea will be proved to be correct. That of course requires a hell of a lot of experimenting which is what students are for.

One of the laws of science (these change every so often so check local press for details) is that whatever idea you have just verified after years of work in the laboratory, a research team at a Midwestern American university has just proved the exact opposite.

Science used to be fun. No one knew anything (they did but not scientifically so it didn't count) so you could just go around proving all sorts of stuff with a notebook and a few test tubes. Now you have to spend seven years glued to a microscope looking up the arse of a fruit fly before you can come to any sort of provisional hypothesis. It would be far better if you could just have the hypothesis and forget the research but then you'd just be a freethinker and there's no room for that kind of heretical behaviour in science.

Scientists have a reputation for dressing poorly and having the social skills of a marrow. This is because they are all engaged in a wider experiment to prove that human interaction is actually unnecessary in the march of scientific progress. If you need to contact these researchers for any reason, they're on the Internet.

Scientists are the monks of the modern world. They are people who know the speed of light but can't count their change. Warning signs that you are becoming a scientist are when you prefer maths with letters rather than numbers, when you find chess sexually arousing and when your idea of a holiday is a symposium.

The central article of faith amongst scientists is that they are making progress. Like every other religion they have an unshakeable belief in a better world to come. Of course we won't know whether that's true until the big scientific experiment is over but by then it will be too late.

How to... appreciate art

Appreciating art is very easy once you understand art history. Art started with two-dimensional cave paintings. Then came two-dimensional church paintings. In the Renaissance artists got perspective and started painting jugs. The Enlightenment brought us well-lit jugs with a side order of fruit. Romantic art depicted the landscape cave dwellers would have seen if they'd looked out of their cave, had perspective and understood lighting.

Art then became what artists saw inside themselves rather than outside. Impressionism was the world seen through a couple of glasses of *vin rouge*. Expressionism was impressionism after the whole bottle. Vorticism was when the room started spinning and modern conceptual art is the throwing-up stage.

A conceptual artist is the purest form of capitalist in that they have no artistic merit until they have sold something. The more they sell, the more talented they become. This kind of art doesn't have to mean anything because there is a professional body of people whose job is to interpret it. The artists install the art, the critics give it meaning and the collectors give it value. It's a great system for everyone concerned except for the general public. But then art is none of their concern.

Figurative art continues to be painted, bought, hung and enjoyed by the vast majority of the population who can't afford artistic good taste. This style of art has four main themes: young boy and girl kissing in meadow; horse ploughing field followed by gulls; small harbour with gaily coloured fishing smacks; deer on misty mountain.

In a traditional gallery it is very impolite to actually look at a painting directly. You wouldn't stare at someone in real life, so why start with a painting. Instead you must give it the briefest of glances and then move on to the label which tells you what it is and who painted it.

There are three important rooms in any gallery that you shouldn't miss. Firstly there are the washrooms. If galleries hung great masters above the urinals they would have more chance of being looked at properly than anywhere else.

Secondly, you must visit the café. When you've failed to be moved by any of the great masters in the galleries, a nice cup of tea and a slice of banana cake will give you that missing sense of spiritual uplift.

Finally, there is the gift shop. This is where you can buy postcards of the great masters so you can actually have a good look at them without being jostled by a

French coach party. You can also buy posters of the great masters to hang up at home which is the modern equivalent of cave painting.

How to... study

Studying is copying things from books and revising is highlighting the nouns in the things you have copied. Remember your teacher has probably written the book you're copying from, although when you have reduced his life's work to one noun he might not recognize it.

There are often a lot of books to get through when you're studying. Fortunately most books are padding and unnecessary wordy stuff. Read the introduction, the conclusion and the chapter headings and you will have the main points. Then pick out one very small fact to give the impression you've pored over every line.

It's impossible to study properly without the correct stationery. Time spent in the stationery shop is therefore every bit as useful as time spent in the library. A decent hole punch can mean the difference between a good university and a poor one.

Nowadays it's possible to study on the Internet. The slight drawback of this is that you're likely to spend 98 per cent of your time looking at things that have nothing to do with your studies. This isn't very helpful for studying but does give a useful insight into what it's going to be like working in an office.

Mnemonics are a vital part of studying as they help you remember things, if that is, you can remember what a mnemonic is in the first place. The best example is Richard of York Gained Battles in Vain which helps you remember how to tell the weather simply by looking at the clouds: Red Overhead You'll Go Blue in a Vest.

To study properly you need to get rid of all distractions. As virtually anything from a small piece of dust upwards can distract from studying, this can take a considerable amount of time. In fact one of the main reasons why people hate studying so much is because it requires so much cleaning, tidying and catering before you can even get started. It's also important to have complete and utter silence when you're studying. The only way to get this is to put your own music on at maximum volume to drown out all the other racket in the house.

Many people take stimulants to help them study longer. Caffeine is the most popular. If you're snorting it straight from the jar, you're probably overdoing it. Go steady with other stimulants in case you find yourself accidentally inventing a new branch of science. Examiners won't be impressed by this as they only know about existing branches.

When you're studying, you may think you're cramming your head with information that will have no use in later life. Nothing could be further from the truth. Your standing in the community is largely judged by your performance in pub quizzes and trivia competitions. And remember, millions can be won or lost on whether you know the name of King John's dog.

How to… do exams

Young people think they know everything. Exams are a way of showing them that this might not actually be the case. One of the best things about being an adult is that you don't have to take any more exams, unless of course you're an accountant. Accountants spend the first half of their life taking exams and the second half marking other people's papers.

For your first two jobs it's vital that you put all your exam results on your CV including the fact that you looked after the school rabbit. After your second job it will count against you if you're still mentioning your GCSEs. Before you get too worried about your results, remember that in the long run no one has their GCSE results on their gravestones (unless they got an A in stonemasonry).

People with office jobs go to great lengths not to take work home. One of the main reasons is so they can spend quality time with their family. Sadly, children do have to bring their work home. It's called homework, which is one of the main reasons they're not available for quality time with the rest of the family.

Revision is foreplay for exams: the more you do the better results you'll get. There are five stages for revision: get a book, skim the book, highlight the good bits, learn the good bits, think of a mnemonic. Mnemonics are funny little words like FRJNAYTOAD which represents the first letter of all the early Roman emperors. Fifty years later when you've forgotten that the Romans even had an empire, you'll still remember FRJNAYTOAD. It's just a shame you can't go into exams write your name, FRJNAYTOAD and then clear off.

If you can forget the work aspect, exams are actually quite interesting. For a start, never again is anybody going to tell you to turn over a piece of paper. During the exam you'll do more handwriting than you will then do in the whole of the rest of your natural life. Finally, exams are the last quizzes you'll ever do relatively sober.

Once the exam is under way don't be put off by other people asking for more paper every two minutes. They're probably taking exams in protecting the environment. Also take time to read the question carefully. If you read it enough times you'll find it's actually asking you the question you revised the answer to and not the one you didn't.

Sadly, the better you do in exams, the more money you're likely to earn for the rest of your life. In fact every hour of revision, at today's prices, is worth £1000 on your final pensionable salary. Therefore if a girl does ten hours of revision a week, calculate when she can afford to retire. You may use calculators and independent financial advisers.

How to... do an evening class

If school days are the best days of your life, then evening classes are the best evenings of your life. This is partly because evenings only become important to people who are past having the best nights of their life. All evening classes stop at 9pm which is the watershed in terms of people being in bed with their cocoa by 10pm. That's why detention is a very real and unpleasant threat in evening classes.

Generally you can choose between vocational classes and leisure classes. For example, very few people do the Chartered Institute of Purchase and Supply (CIPS) Graduate Diploma for fun. Similarly very few people do an Introduction to Fungi for vocational reasons. Although if you did both you might have a bright future as a supermarket mushroom buyer.

Many evening classes take place in schools and colleges and you can do things you never did when you were there the first time like listen and pay attention. There are other things that you'll find very difficult to do again, for example putting up your hand and saying,

'Me, please miss.' Although for some men this is the sole reason they do evening classes.

The teacher is a vital part of evening classes. If you're lucky you can get a retired professor and world expert in the subject. Generally you get a person who did the course last time and now considers himself to be a professor and world expert.

One of the most shocking aspects of evening classes is when you are given homework to do. This eats into your valuable leisure time when you could be doing things like sitting slumped in the sofa rotting like a vegetable.

It's always nice to have someone in your class you fancy a little bit. Pick your class carefully as there are unlikely to be many men in the Level Two Certificate of Nail Treatment. On the other hand, if you are a man, Level Two Certificate of Nail Treatment is a good bet. Although they probably won't let you on the course unless you have Level One.

Learning a language is a very popular evening class. Beginner classes take about thirty weeks to say 'Hello, my name is Brian.' That's why it's only after the first twenty-eight weeks you realize that you're in Modern Greek rather than German for Business.

The best thing about evening classes is when you take an exam at the end and you pass it with distinction. But perhaps the most depressing thing is when your parents don't want to see your certificate in Practical Plant

Propagation because, firstly, they thought they'd educated you enough and, secondly, they're both in a home.

How to... be a musician

Classical musicians tend to be either rather saintly or rather godlike. It all depends on how much weight they have to carry around. Double bassists are always humble because they've been given a massive double-bass-shaped cross to bear. Violinists are quite cocky because they've only got hand luggage, but worst of all are conductors who have nothing to carry but an oversized toothpick.

In classical music, instruments are divided into four rather sexual categories: blowing, scratching, fingering and banging. There is also a further specialized category of beating with a stick. No correlation exists between musical and sexual performance except for the fact that 90 per cent of musicians instinctively make love in three-eight time.

During security scares police often check lock-up garages. The thing they find most of are musicians rehearsing. Musicians' rehearsals follow the same trajectory as mental illness: you start in the warmth of a loving home and increasingly find yourself out in the cold or in a small soundproof room.

Parents usually choose the instrument you play first. That's why you see so few child bassoonists. If there were a totally silent instrument it would probably be a winner with most parents. Parents also put you through your grades. Grade One means you can hold your instrument, Grade Two means you can get a noise out of it and Grade Three means you can get a recognizable noise. Anything above requires an ability to play properly which is when most young people transfer to football or snogging.

You can tell how good people are at music by how much their bodies move. In the beginning the body is held in an absolute rictus of concentration while the search is on for middle C. Later on the body relaxes as the fingers do most of the work. Once the fingers do what you want instinctively, the whole body gets back into the act by weaving, swaying and sweating.

In the long run the instrument you choose to play is an accurate reflection of you as a person. For example, no one who plays the tuba is ever treated for depression. Similarly people who play the oboe tend to have complex love lives and piccolo players are often negligent with their tax returns.

Where you hold your instrument also has a bearing on the music. Violins are held like a finger on the chin which is why the music tends to be rather thoughtful. Cellists put their instrument between their legs which is why they're earthy and sensual. Trumpeters stand like somebody telling a joke at a bar which is why their music often sounds like loud laughter. Bagpipes don't bear thinking about.

How to... do maths

Maths is the purest science in that you don't need any test tubes or animal testing to do it. All the other sciences eventually boil down to maths, apart from biology which boils down to soup. There are two types of maths: maths with numbers and maths with letters. Don't try the one with letters when you're checking your change in the pub.

Doing maths with letters makes as much sense as painting with numbers. Actually painting with numbers makes a surprising amount of sense and you can get a very nice picture of the *Cutty Sark*. Funnily enough you can also paint with figures but let's not complicate matters. After all maths is about simplicity, discovering the beautiful equations that underpin nature such as 1+1 = 1 (unless you have twins).

Mathematicians like letters a lot and they have their special favourites. Chief amongst these are a and b and x and y. Interestingly, you never see much of w. This is because it features the word 'double' which means times by two and would easily confuse mathematicians.

In the real world, when letters meet numbers, you get a bus route. In maths, you get an equation. With these equations mathematicians can work out the distance to the planets, the direction of evolution and the mind of God. They miss their bus but that's the price you pay for hot math action.

Of course calculators have made maths much easier for most people, except for professional mathematicians. Because they use letters for maths they can only get their calculators to give them the Spanish word for 'police station'.

Mathematicians have a lot of the trainspotter about them and for them the primes are the *Flying Scotsman* of numbers. Prime numbers are irregular, odd and never quite what they appear to be: hence Prime Minister.

Given the importance of maths, it's surprising that there are only ten numbers to choose from. It's rumoured that a new number between four and five was discovered in the fifties but that it was hushed up in case they had to start the decade again with the new number.

The four horsemen of mathematics are multiplication, division, addition and subtraction. There is also a fifth thing you can do with figures and that is announce them. This is the favoured option of politicians and it supersedes all other mathematical rules.

In the old days fractions were the high point of mathematics and only one third of school leavers were comfortable with them. Thanks to the recent advances in education that is now up to 25 per cent of school leavers, according to recently announced government figures.

Maps and Roads

How to… parallel park

Everyone can remember where they were when Diana died. Everyone can also remember where they were when they did the perfect parallel park, when they got into a space with four inches to spare at either end, first time and flush with the kerb. If you ever wanted to commit a perfect crime, right after your perfect parallel parking would be good because there are never any witnesses. Instead it's an iron rule of nature that the tightest spaces come complete with four witnesses in your car bent on personal humiliation.

Judging the space you need is very easy; if you're by yourself in a quiet street, no gap's too narrow; if your partner is in the passenger seat you need enough room to park a mobile home and trailer; if you're in a crowded shopping centre and a crowd gathers as soon as you select reverse, the gap's far, far too small and you'd be much better off parking somewhere else.

Once you've started your manoeuvre, you soon get into the jimmying back and forth phase where you do a full lock and then move forward two inches. You can be what you think is inches away from the car in front when a family of four with a twin buggy crosses between you. The fail-safe way of making sure you don't hit other cars is to move slowly until you hit something solid; you then know for certain it's time to move in the other direction.

When you're parking near shops, a useful thing to remember is that you can see exactly how much room you have to play with by checking the reflection in the window. Be careful with this especially if you're outside a shoe shop where you can be so transfixed by the strappy little number in the window that you take the plates of a vintage Mercedes behind you.

Everyone knows that you can't parallel park head first – everyone that is who doesn't have a four-wheel-drive vehicle that can mount a kerb a foot high and drop back into position with a satisfying wump. So what if you mow down a group of passing pedestrians and their dog. If you drive an off-road vehicle it's obvious that you're going to be driving off road from time to time and they should bear that in mind.

In Hollywood movies you'll see all sorts of fancy driving and car chases but you'll never see parallel parking. That's because stunt drivers, like everyone else in the world, can't do it. The other reason is that America has decided that one of the constitutional rights of its citizens should be freedom from parallel parking and use of mirrors and reverse gear.

When you're getting into a tight spot you need every

spare inch. Don't be shy of nudging the car in front of you. After all that's what bumpers are for. Just be sure that your bumpers are at the same level. You don't want to shoot back in reverse and discover a pair of bull bars through your back window. The trick is to aim for your rear lights to kiss the headlights of the person behind you. This is a light kiss not the sort of kiss that leaves shattered teeth all over the road.

How to... give clear directions

It's worrying to think that at any given time 25 per cent of road users aren't really sure where they're going. What's even more chilling is that when you stop for directions, 90 per cent of people you ask haven't a clue where you're going but nevertheless give full instructions on how to get there.

Foreigners get lost easily and often ask for directions. They pull up, wind the window down and ask, 'Where is Mercers Road?', whereupon two things happen: you realize that you've never heard of Mercers Road and they realize that they don't speak English. In an ideal world you would say, 'I don't know', they would say 'I don't understand' and then they would drive off and everyone would be happy.

Instead you give directions to anywhere you can think of that a foreigner would be likely to be going at that time of day and they nod in a painful way and wonder what this 'roundabout' is you mention so often. Finally, with much embarrassment all round they roar off up a cul-de-sac and then drive back past you three minutes later slumped so low in their seats it looks as if no one is driving.

An amazing thing happens when you ask for directions from someone. You immediately start nodding and stop listening. When you drive off you both say, 'What did he say?' and you realize that neither of you heard a word he said but you both noticed his luxuriant nasal hair. Even if you do listen, it's impossible to take in any road directions with more than three elements. People can only absorb left, right, straight over – after that your mental road map goes blank.

Remember when you ask directions that you're speaking to a pedestrian who is thinking like a pedestrian. When they say second right, third left, you'll be counting tarmaced signposted roads, they'll be counting bridleways and holes in hedges which is why where you want to go is fifty yards away and where you end up is fifty miles away.

If you're asking for directions, never pick on people who look starved of social interaction. As they never go anywhere they won't know how to get anywhere but that won't stop them having an hour-long conversation, reading your entire atlas with you, settling down in your back seat and helping themselves to your flask of coffee.

How to... navigate

During the war all road signs were removed to confuse German invaders. If fact half those missing in action in the war were people who had trouble getting home on leave and had to pretend they'd always meant to resettle in Swindon.

Navigation is not easy even with road signs. Many marriages falter shortly after someone says, 'I'll drive, you navigate.' Men believe that all women lack the essential DNA for navigation. They've watched their partners veer aimlessly all over shopping centres with no clear sense of purpose or direction and they fear that this will be the same on major roads.

Most people have a big road atlas in the car. The reason they are so big and floppy is in the interests of safety; when a man says to a woman, 'The blue one's a motorway not a river,' he is a split second away from getting a *1998 Motorists' Atlas* full in the face. Hardback atlases can cause major structural damage when swung at speed.

You can tell a good navigator by their anticipation.

Ideally you'll get, 'In half a mile take the turning on your left marked A420.' Any instruction that starts with 'We should have…' is not good. If you're married to this kind of navigator it's wise not to let them near Ordnance Survey maps unless you enjoy a nice country walk attempting to follow the 'path' of a line of pylons.

Inevitably, on a long journey in unfamiliar territory, a wrong turn will be made. If a woman takes a wrong turn this is because she has the direction-finding capacity of an old shopping trolley. If a man takes a wrong turning it's because it's an ingenious short cut. It may be a special kind of short cut that seems to be longer than a long cut but this shouldn't be mentioned until you both have grandchildren and life has lost some of its intensity.

Women have advanced psychological weapons for use with navigation. For example, if they take a wrong turn it is actually the man's fault because he passed up the opportunity for correcting her at the appropriate moment. When men get their directional knickers twisted they often drop into the silent rally driver from hell mode where they think that they will be able to make up for a colossal map-reading error by driving like a loony for half an hour.

One useful tip in navigation is that there are no sets of identical villages in this country. When you've just gone through the same village twice it means that she took the wrong turning, his short cut was a circle and someone is in line for the *1998 Motorists' Atlas* in the face treatment.

How to... buy a new car

Buying a new car is clearly a big decision. You need to do a lot of detailed research comparing urban cycle mpg, depreciation costs and load carrying capacity across a wide range of cars. And then when you've finished all this research you get the car you fancied in the first place even if it has the mpg of an armoured personnel carrier and the depreciation of a dot.com share.

It's always a good idea to test drive a new car. It's called a test drive because you suddenly feel like you're doing your driving test again. The ten minutes you have in the car will be the worst ten minutes of driving you've done since you were with your dad in Sainsbury's car park. It doesn't help that the salesman will be pointing out the superb road holding as you accidentally mount a kerb because you can't find the clutch. It's much better just to sit in the driver's seat in the showroom, hold the wheel tightly and make quiet vrooming noises.

At some stage the salesman might lift the bonnet for you to have a look at the engine. It's very difficult to know what to say at this stage as you feel as if a waiter has taken you to have a look at the kitchen. Just say something like, 'So that's where they put it' and then ask to see something useful like how you get the filler cap off.

There are some sharp practices in car sales and one of the worst is cut and shut where two halves of old cars are welded together. Look out for subtle little signs such as the front half of the car being a Ford Escort and the back a Vauxhall Viva. It's easy to spot dodgy second-hand car places because they are obliged by law to put up those little lines of blue, red and white flags. Just think of these as the equivalent of 'Police Line – Do Not Cross' ribbons around the site of an attempted robbery.

When you're inspecting a car some people think kicking the tyres is a good idea. This does two things: it tells the vendor that you know nothing about cars and tells you that your shoes aren't as thick as you thought they were. Kicking the body panels is strictly forbidden and you can actually be prosecuted for vandalism.

If you're worried about a car you can always get a reputable motoring organization to come out and have a look at the car for you. If the cost of this check is more than the price of the car you might want to think whether this is a smart move.

How to... survive a long car journey

Never attempt to make a long journey in a car without an ample supply of boiled sweets in the glove compartment. An average size butterscotch, driven at a constant 70mph, will last for almost twenty-five miles, or two if you crunch it. When you are travelling with your partner make sure they have sweets to suit them. Discovering that your beloved has only brought pineapple chunks for a drive from Perth to London can put considerable strain on the relationship.

Check all levels before you go: oil, water, petrol and bladder. Again the standard rule here is that most people average two bladders' worth to a tank of petrol. Naturally, emptying and filling rarely coincide which is why the nation's hedgerows are under chemical siege. Always make sure you've got your favourite tapes with you. These you can listen to in the three minutes your partner is behind a hedge before they get back in, berate you for your taste in music, and then demand to listen to the radio instead.

Children need feeding on a long journey. Make sure

you prepare a nice packed lunch for them but on no account park in the McDonalds car park to eat it. The curse of travelling with a family is thc question, 'Are we nearly there yet?', which is generally asked for the first time at the end of the road where you live. This is where the butterscotches come in handy. Preferably five at a time.

Some cars have a built-in entertainment system where the kids in the back seat have a wide range of interesting games in front of them. In newer cars this is a games console, in older cars it's the back of the driver's head. There are a number of other interesting and fun games for children. In the old days a perennial favourite used to be spot the funny foreign-made car. Now's it spot the funny British-made car, or spot the foreign-made car with a relatively large input of British components and labour. If you live in the south-east another excellent game is spot the piece of road without a car on it.

Road atlases come into their own on long journeys, which is why it's sensible not to keep them in the boot. Over the years manufacturers of road atlases have been involved in a size war with the result that an open road atlas is now the same width as your windscreen. On the other hand you have to beware of much smaller, hard-back road atlases that came from your grandmother's Triumph Herald. They're much handier but they don't have any motorways in them and all the roads lead to Stonehenge.

How to... wait for a bus

Waiting for a bus is an art. Conversations should be limited to, 'It's late this morning.' Anything more and you'll end up having that person sitting next to you and showing you their eczema. Form an orderly queue and remember that this is the order you get on the bus. Even if the bus doors open at the back of the queue, you must do a little snaking manoeuvre to get the front of the queue on first. It's always first come, first served and anything else is throwing out two thousand years of civilization.

Waiting for the school bus in winter is just about the only toughening-up outdoor activity children get these days. Their parents might send them out in a nice duffel coat to keep them as warm as toast but, as far as coolness is concerned, most kids would rather throw themselves under a bus than wear it. That's why kids have such big sports bags – to carry all the scarves, mittens and thermal underwear their mothers send them out in.

On the other hand, adults dress up nice and warmly for the twenty-minute wait, the bus comes early, they make a mad dash for it and they end up sitting in their own dripping sauna. That's why buses in the winter all smell like the drying room of a youth hostel.

Looking for the bus actually stops it coming; the driver is waiting around the corner and he simply won't budge until you stop constantly looking for him. The only way to guarantee it coming is to be at the exact point where you know that, unless you're Linford Christie, running for it is absolutely futile.

Hailing a bus requires shoving your arm out in an aggressive, assertive manner entirely alien to the British character and most people would rather miss several buses than be accused of being too fascistic in their arm movements. Teenagers, who are physically incapable of moving their arms higher than their waists, can't hail buses full stop. Fortunately they are in such big clumps of sullenness that you can't really miss them if you're a bus driver. Especially if you aim straight for them.

Of course, this all assumes that your bus comes. Sometimes buses just don't come and they don't come three at once either. This is a myth put about by bus companies to pretend that there's actually more than one bus serving your route. If you really want a frequent bus service, you need to live in Not in Service which is choked with buses pretty much all the time.

How to... use a taxi

There are generally two types of taxis in service: the first are cabs that smell of essence of vanilla and are owned by the driver; the second are cabs that smell of the compost of humanity and are rented by the driver. Taxi drivers also fall into two types: those who talk in a friendly way at the beginning of the journey because they like talking and those who talk in a friendly way at the end of the journey because they like tipping.

When you're sitting in the back of a taxi and talking to a cabbie you have to decide whether to look at the back of the driver's neck or at his eyes in the rear-view mirror. If you do a bit of both you come away with the spooky impression that the driver has eyes in the back of his head. You also realize that you've been driven the whole way by someone staring into the rear-view mirror.

Backs of cabs are a fantastic place to pounce on the person you fancy. It's relatively private but not so private that you can't immediately stop, get out and be public again. (Interestingly, a good snog lasts about £1.60 on the meter of a black cab.)

Hailing a cab is often awkward for the British who have been trained from birth not to flap their arms around like excitable continentals. Ideally cabbies would notice when you did a cool little flicking movement with your hand. In reality the cabbie will be mesmerized by the man on the other side of the street doing the impression of a heron taking off.

The last quarter of any taxi journey is spent praying the meter will stop on an amount that allows you to give one note and say a breezy, 'Keep the change.' Cabbies are wise to this and will drive a route guaranteed to finish when the fare is five pence over the note forcing you to give a cripplingly large tip.

Being driven around in the back of a cab is the nearest most of us will get to the sensation of being royal. The only difference is that taxis don't have police outriders so you'll probably be stuck in traffic waving at the same person for five minutes. You also won't have people waving back at you except for the idiots who are trying to hail the cab because they haven't noticed you in it.

British cab drivers are famous the world over for their detailed knowledge of the streets and of every political and social issue under the sun. Unlicensed minicab drivers also know the streets except the streets will be those of their home city ten thousand miles away. You can always give them directions. Sadly this is not always possible after a good night out, when finding the door of the cab is as much as you can manage unaided.

How to... fill up

Petrol stations have been carefully designed so that whichever way you approach them, your filler cap will be on the opposite side to the pump. In order to cope with this fact the pumps have special extendible hoses that stretch right over the top of your car and stop two inches short of the hole.

When it comes to technique, filling up and sex have a lot in common. Once you've got the nozzle firmly stuck in, pace is everything. Pumps have two speeds. The first is incredibly slow so that by the time you're nearly full, you've got frostbite in your fingers, cramp up your entire arm and seven cars waiting. The other speed is supergush which kicks in when you attempt to put the last ten pence worth in to round it up to the twenty pounds.

In the old days petrol stations used to sell petrol. If you were lucky they might also sell a big bag of Opal Fruits. Nowadays many petrol stations are mini-supermarkets, newsagents and coffee shops all rolled into one. Indeed, if they had somewhere to put a sleeping bag they would be the ideal locations for a weekend minibreak.

Petrol stations are also the natural habitat of the Cornish pasty. This isn't surprising as the pasty grew up with the mining industry and has always had a close association with fossil fuels. Indeed in its own scalloped way, the pasty is a fossil fuel. Often there is a microwave provided to heat the pasty up and a bin to throw it in on your way out.

Loos in filling stations used to have a very bad reputation. At first they didn't exist at all, then they existed but were locked and finally they were open but out of order. Now they're checked every two minutes by a member of staff, generally while you're in the middle of getting your nozzle out.

When you pay for your petrol it's important to remember two things. Firstly you need to know what pump you filled up at. If you're in Cumbria that's easy because there's only one pump in Cumbria. If you're in a forecourt with lots of pumps and you've forgotten the number, then you'll probably remember the amount because you're the embarrassing gusher at £20.01.

You also need to continually remind yourself that you don't need another atlas. For a man there is nothing quite so sexy as a big *Road Atlas* with next year's date on. The fact that 0.0001 per cent of the roads will have changed is more than enough justification for getting one. Men know that in a bizarre and inexplicable way, the older your *Road Atlas* is, the slower you drive.

How to... drive a hire car

Picking up a hire car in a strange country recreates the exact feeling of your first driving lesson: you're left alone with the steering wheel on the wrong side of the car, the car on the wrong side of the road and your seat adjusted for a midget with no apparent means of moving it back. When you finally have the courage to move off, you try to indicate left and the windscreen wipers go on, when you want the windscreen wipers, you put the headlights on, and when you want the headlights, the boot opens.

On the plus side you will already be familiar with the concept of a clutch unless you are an American for whom changing gear is what you do in a clothes shop. Even better you won't have your father in the passenger seat shouting at you to check your mirrors and assuming the brace position every time you get into second gear. After half an hour or so of continuous driving in your hire car, you generally build up enough confidence to leave the car park.

Eventually, after about fifty miles or so of driving, you

become accustomed to the local driving conditions such as synchronized horn and hand gestures. You then enter the most dangerous phase of driving abroad where you get ever so slightly cocky. It's generally at that precise moment that you turn the wrong way into a sixteen-lane express way.

Just when you master the driving, you have to fill up with petrol. Getting the petrol cap off a strange car is akin to taking its virginity. With some cars you can't even get the flap open let alone the cap off. And once you finally get at the cap, they often have devious little locks and odd twisting mechanisms that would have commanded a hefty premium fitted on medieval chastity belts. Eventually after pushing, pulling and twisting everything that moves inside and out of the car, you find a handy little lever in exactly the same place as the one in your car at home.

It would be much easier if you didn't have to fill up at all, but hire companies insist you return the car with the tank full. This is a slightly strange concept as it's like being asked to return your beer glass to the bar as full as when you got it. Make sure you don't fill up at any station within a one-mile radius of the hire-car depot. They know you're desperate and will charge for petrol at a rate which makes drilling for your own oil a serious economic alternative.

How to... drive on motorways

There are three speeds on motorways, fast, faster and 'For God's sake slow down Brian'. Safe driving is easy if you follow the golden rule of the highway code: manoeuvre, mirror, hand signal. Getting off a motorway is simple because the exits are helpfully numbered and are easy to spot especially for the drivers of the five big lorries that suddenly get between you and the sign at the crucial moment.

Service stations are spaced at exactly the time it takes for a cup of tea to pass through your digestive system plus half an hour. Many people make the mistake of relaxing after turning into a service station. This is when you take the wrong lane that puts you straight back onto the motorway just as your bladder muscle becomes totally relaxed.

Some people drive incredibly close behind you and nothing you can do will shake them off. Eventually you realize that you've got your rear-view mirror badly adjusted and the person tailgating you is actually your granddad sitting quietly in the back seat.

On motorways they now have big illuminated signs saying, 'Tiredness Can Kill. Take a Break.' Most people are too tired to read these signs or, if they do read them, take their eyes off the road just as a tanker lorry cuts in front of them. More effective signs would say something like, 'Slow down, Brian, you're driving like an idiot.' All Brians would definitely take notice and everyone who wasn't Brian would be on the look out for this madman.

Motorway driving is fairly dull and it's a great time to chat away on your mobile phone. This must be done hands-free as by law your hands must be available for eating your sandwiches, reading your atlas, clipping your toenails and so forth.

Interestingly, 12 per cent of the total radio output in the country is traffic reports. These reports are divided into letting you know that you're currently sitting in a big jam and telling you of minute traffic incidents at the far end of the country that aren't even affecting the people involved. All traffic reports work on the flawed premise that there's an alternative to being on the road you're on. Unless you grew up within three miles of the jam, and know the locality intimately, there isn't.

They say that speed and tiredness are the big killers on motorways. They only say this because it actually sounds silly to say that Abba tapes and Imperial Mints are the big killers. But they definitely are because the tape player is what you're looking at and the glove compartment is what you're reaching for when you depart this world.

Planning and Action

How to... clear the decks

Every now and then your body has a strange urge to eat something fresh. Your mind sometimes has a similar urge to make things fresh by clearing the decks.

Deck clearance is actually very hard work. It requires all sorts of physical shifting and mental concentration. The good news is that the job you're clearing the decks for is unlikely to be as taxing. The bad news is that you'll be too exhausted to do it.

It's important that you don't take clearing the decks too far and get involved in a whole new decking project. You're supposed to be clearing the decks for new work, not making work by creating new decks.

One drawback of clearing the decks is that you can get addicted to clear decks. This inevitably leads to obsessive tidying until you're sitting on the floor in an empty room with your entire life on a slim laptop.

It's far more difficult to clear the emotional decks and get rid of the relationship debris that is cluttering up your life. Interestingly, the same techniques of binning paper-work (old letters) and moving things round (furniture they've used) works wonders. As does ripping up the decks completely and burning them while chanting ancient curses.

For many people, clearing the deck means clearing the desk. The easiest way of clearing your desk is to fill your drawers. If you look at people with neat desks they often have just as much paper on them as people with messy desks. The secret is they put their papers in exceptionally neat piles which then look like one piece of paper.

If you're really keen you can then go through this pile and take actions. Your paperwork will either have matured like wine and be ready for ingestion or it will have matured like milk and will no longer be fit for human consumption.

Decks are mostly cluttered by things you've been meaning to do. Funnily enough you get more satisfaction out of doing things you've been meaning to do than things you have to do. That's because the moral victory is greater. Once you've done all the things you've been meaning to do, you're then frighteningly exposed to all the things you've never thought of doing and which could change your life.

Clearing the decks means doing things you previously chose not to do. In effect you are entering a parallel universe of previously rejected possibilities. As one thing leads on to another you may find yourself changing the whole future course of your life. On the other hand, that just sounds like a pathetic excuse not to tidy up.

How to... change your life

Any fool can chuck in their job, sell their house and sail off to the four corners of the earth. However, you're not really changing your life, you're just chucking in your job, selling your house and running away to the four corners of the earth and you'll still be the same old idiot doing it.

A much more profound change is having grapefruit for breakfast. Inviting fruit into your life, especially at breakfast when you're at your weakest, is a much more difficult challenge especially if you decide to wave goodbye to your sausage at the same time.

Changing what you wear can also completely change your life. For example, if you've spent the last ten years in thick corduroy trousers and then decide to go out and buy a pair of cargo pants, you're suddenly going to feel very uncomfortable with folk music and ancient battle re-enactments.

Dramatic haircuts in both men and women are often an outward and visible sign of an inward and spiritual shift. By applying this psychology in reverse, you can often trigger a shift in outlook by changing your hairstyle; for example, give yourself a side parting and notice how your shoes begin to look shinier and how the urge to pull your socks up acquires a strange intensity.

If you regularly disagree with someone, try agreeing with them for while. This is extremely unnerving for them and also gives you the moral high ground which is a lovely place with great views. Changing partners is a good way of changing your life but should be approached with care. Partners, like pants, should only be changed when not to change them becomes absolutely unthinkable.

Every night half the population looks through the TV listings and decides there's absolutely nothing on. The other half of the population looks at the same list and thinks it's TV Heaven. Swap halves and watch all their stuff. Once you get into the stride of changing your life it takes on its own momentum. For example, not only are you on a different train to work but you're also facing backwards and reading bits of the paper you've never noticed before.

Of course many of us are creatures of habit; we know exactly what we like and we make sure we stay well inside our comfort zone. Just remember that there's always somewhere more comfortable than your comfort zone and eventually that thought will make you so uncomfortable you'll venture out of your current comfort zone.

Or you may not. You may in fact have your life so well ordered that you don't want to do or change anything. Technically, however, you're not actually living and, if your heart and mind were linked to a monitor, you'd be flat-lining. So unless you quite like the sound of being part of the living dead, reach for the grapefruit.

How to… pull yourself together

There are some days, many of them in February, where everything is so miserable and depressing that you can feel all your energy, confidence and self-respect disappearing over the horizon with its arse on fire. You then have a choice: either you can immediately book yourself a four-month holiday in the Caribbean or, if that's not possible for some reason, you can pull yourself together.

The difficulty is that when you're feeling glum the last thing you want to do is to pull yourself anywhere. The only thing you want to pull is the phone out of the wall, the top off a bottle of gin and the duvet over your head.

Oddly, when you're feeling low the first instinct is to do a whole range of things that immediately make you feel worse; you sleep with someone 90 per cent unsuitable for the 10 per cent comfort factor; you go shopping for clothes which are 90 per cent overpriced and 10 per cent suitable and then you eat a catering tub of ice cream which makes you feel 90 per cent sick and 10 per cent depressed. You then don't go to a party because you feel so miserable and then you wonder why no one phones you (they're all at the party).

When you feel glum you think that the world is an awful place, that everything in it is conspiring against you and that never has one person suffered so much. Try standing in front of a mirror, repeating that to yourself and see if you can keep a straight face. If you can, then put yourself through the following emergency de-glumming programme.

Firstly, get moving. Either take your dog for a walk so long it thinks it's auditioning for a remake of *The Incredible Journey*, or go to the gym and test your lycra to destruction. When you get in, put a load of washing on, make something large and hot to eat, wash up all your dirty dishes, tidy up the whole house, throw lots of old things away, pour yourself a large drink and then look through your photo album to remind you of the good times. (Don't do this if you generally look like a dork in photos.)

Then have another large drink, put your favourite CD on at an unethically high volume and dance around like an idiot until you collapse with exhaustion. And finally, when you get into bed, remember however bad things are, they're a lot worse in other parts of the world. Except in the Caribbean of course.

How to… live with keys

When you were eighteen you used to be given the keys to the house. Nowadays this is the age when your parents are most likely to change the locks.

In the dish at home that sits in the drawer full of rubbish in your kitchen, there will be a selection of mystery, unlabelled keys. If you really want to know what they unlock, throw them all away and in a matter of hours you will find out.

Carrying a bunch of keys has always been a bit of nightmare unless you carry a handbag or you're a beefeater or both. That's why people with expensive suits like to holster up their keys in a little leather pouchette. However, be aware that the best way of signalling to your partner that it's time to leave a dull party is to jangle your keys in an imminent departure kind of way and you can't jangle a little leather pouchette.

The greatest fear of people who live by themselves is that they will leave the house without their keys. That's why the first thing they do when they've closed the door behind them is to check for their keys. Alternatively they leave their keys with a neighbour who can be trusted. The golden rule here is if your neighbour doesn't immediately entrust you with their keys in return then they are not to be trusted.

Many people choose to hide their keys. The top places are under the mat, under the dustbin or in a place so secure that you've completely wiped it from your memory. Some people like to carry their bunch of keys on their belt loop. The reason for this is that the one thing you're least likely to forget when you walk out of the house is your trousers.

Everyone has a few big old shed keys with one tooth which all look interchangeable but aren't. The reason why the key that looks remarkably like your shed key doesn't unlock the shed is because the key that is your shed key doesn't open the shed either. The whole point of keys is that no two keys are the same, that's why it's foolish of you to expect that the key you got copied from your front door key will actually open your front door.

One day keys may be replaced by smart cards but not until the cards are smart enough to get themselves into your back pocket when you've just strode out of the house without them. Biometrics will mean the end of all keys smart or stupid. You'll simply roll up to your house, shout 'It's me' and the lock will completely ignore you like your girlfriend would in a similar situation.

How to... manage your money

There are all sorts of attractive, tax-efficient homes for your money. Most of them are small offshore islands but these are only for people who have too much money to pay tax. For the rest of the population there are things called ISAs, TESSAs and PEPs. These will be explained to you by an IFA or Independent Financial Adviser. They're independent because they've made so much money knowing more about your money than you do.

Many people are still suspicious of financial institutions and prefer to keep their money in a shoebox on top of their wardrobe. The advantages are the high rate of interest in that there's nothing quite so interesting as counting through a wad of greasy tenners. The disadvantages are that it is also an instant access account for the local drug addict.

Pensions are basically your pay packet for when you no longer get a pay packet. Ideally, to give yourself a decent pension, you should have started paying into one seventy years ago. By the time you retire you are paying almost your entire salary into your pension. After you retire, your pension becomes your entire salary. In the old days it was simpler – you paid into a pension all your life and then the day after you retired you died. That's how the pension schemes made their money.

Many people who have children or dependants like to take out insurance to protect their family in the event of their death. The downside of having massive insurance policies on your life is that you can never have another bath without the nagging fear that your spouse is about to drop a toaster in it.

Credit cards are identity cards for the greedy and stupid. They're a great way of ruining your life in easy monthly instalments. When you've messed up your life with six or seven credit cards you can then consolidate your stupidity into one big loan which could actually reduce your overall monthly stupidity.

Most people have bank accounts these days. These are useful for handling bills, standing orders, direct debits, etc. Others prefer to cut out the middleman and give their entire earnings straight to their children.

Many people take their financial planning very seriously. They have a little notebook with neatly ruled columns itemizing every ingoing and outgoing down to the last penny. This is remarkably effective as it takes up so much time it prevents you getting out to actually spend anything.

The people who are best at managing their money are those with lots of money and those with virtually no money. That's because if you've got everything you don't need anything and if you've got nothing you can't afford anything. It's the people who can afford things they don't need who are really in trouble.

How to... make a decision

In life there are no such things as decisions. Instead there are attempts to stand up and surf on the rolling tide of inevitability. Catching a wave gives the impression that you've made the right decision. Making a bad decision is when you miss a wave, fall off, get whacked on the head by your board, swallow half the ocean and then realize that huge crowds on the beach have watched you make a complete arse of yourself.

When something goes wrong in life you can always trace it back to a decision having been made by someone somewhere. That's why many people avoid making any sort of decision altogether. Interestingly, procrastination is actually the most intensive form of decision making because instead of making one decision and getting it over with, you have to make a decision every five minutes to put off the big decision.

There are three kinds of decisions: proactive, reactive and radioactive. Proactive decisions are the ones you make to give the impression that you're in full command of your destiny. When things go pear-shaped because you made the wrong decision, you can then make more decisions about how to get out of the mess. So long as you keep making a continual stream of decisions, people will think you know what you're doing.

Reactive decision makers take the view that change is inevitable so why rush to meet it. By the time change gets to you the decisions will have been made already so you might as well relax and enjoy it. The only thing you have to do is to identify the decision makers so that blame can be apportioned when necessary.

Radioactive decisions are big decisions made by other people at a distance and you only realize you've been affected by them when it's far too late; these kind of decisions are found a lot in the manufacturing industry, pensions, local government and hospitals.

Making a decision involves taking responsibility. However, responsibility moves at about one tenth of the speed of decision making and as long as you don't wait around to see the consequences of your decisions, you can generally keep well ahead of the responsibility. Or you can simply let other people take responsibility for your actions and claim permanent victim status.

In general, people make decisions because they believe this will keep them on the straight and narrow road to a better future. In reality, life moves round in circles. Decisions you take now are likely to be right in the short term, wrong in the medium term and then right again in the long term. Of course, this could all be rubbish. It's up to you to decide.

How to… plan

The best way to plan is to carefully write everything down on a piece of paper and then rip the paper to shreds. This accurately reflects what happens to plans in real life.

You can't start planning unless you've got a blank sheet of paper and a pen. You then need some peace and quiet and probably a cup of coffee. Several chocolate digestives are required if you're really going to take planning seriously. Often the first part of the subsequent detailed plan is a trip to the shops for more chocolate digestives.

Most people do their planning after the event. This is a lot easier because you know exactly what happened and can come up with a very impressive plan that would have made you look terrific had you actually done any of it.

Planning shouldn't be confused with preparation. Once you've drawn out a really nice plan and got it looking exactly how you want it, you've probably used up all the time for preparation.

People plan all sorts of things including their career, their life and their family. Career planning is like family planning: it's only when you don't do it that things happen. Occasionally people map out an exact plan for every aspect of their life. Interestingly, no one ever plans to underachieve. You won't find many plans that say single, broke and depressed by forty. Maybe that's because this doesn't take much planning.

When you're not part of your own plan, the danger is that you'll end up as part of someone else's. To avoid this you need to plan what you're going to change, how you're going to change it and who's going to get well and truly rogered. Planning is a lot more exciting when you view it as plotting.

The essence of planning is thinking before doing. In today's busy world thinking frightens people and if you stop to do it too often you may find yourself in a home. To protect ourselves we have do something instead of thinking. That's how the list was born.

There are in fact three ways of planning. Writing a list, drawing a diagram and daydreaming. These are related in that points higher than four on a list only get done in your dreams. Similarly, people are very good at drawing up exceptionally complex organization diagrams but then the first thing that actually happens is that you start colouring them in to look nicer.

All politics comes down to planning. If you instinctively plan for yourself you're a capitalist whereas if you instinctively plan for other people you're a socialist. That's why if you want a job for life, become a planner. In fact you should put that in your life plan.

How to... make a list

The world is divided into those people who can't do anything without making a list first, and dangerous anarchists. Writing lists is all about imposing order on a chaotic universe. A dictionary is a list of words, a timetable is a list of trains and an Argos catalogue is a list of the entire artefacts of Western civilization.

The brain can only cope with three items of information at any given moment. Therefore lists start with a minimum of four items. The best lists have ten items on them – ten items are far too many to remember and certainly too many to do at once. Hence the Ten Commandments.

For some people the 'To Do' list is a comfort blanket. Many people actually write down things they've already done on their 'To Do' list so that they can immediately cross them off and get the feeling that they're well on top of things. Other people keep their 'To Do' lists for years so that it always looks 99 per cent completed with one or two minor things to do at the bottom. Remember, it's been statistically proven that by the time you've written a 'To Do' list, you could have done one of the things on the list.

Lists go up and down rather than across, except in Chinese where they go from side to side. This allows you to put things in order and have a top ten. Indeed the amazing popularity of football has nothing to do with the striking of an inflated bladder with the foot, but more to do with the detailed and fascinating lists called League Tables.

There's nothing like seeing your name on a list to make you feel as though you've made it (unless it's a list of the dead). Most people want to be on a list and preferably right at the top. If you're generally nowhere near the top of anything, it's worth remembering that the bottom of one list is always the top of another list. Even if you have to turn the original list upside down.

If you can't be on a list then a good alternative is to be the person who writes the list. This gives you a lot of power and you can say things like, 'Sorry, you're not on my list.' Because not being on a list can often get in your way in life, it's a good idea to always carry around your own official-looking list on which you and your friends feature prominently.

Getting on a list is hard but getting off a list is even harder, as anyone who has ever been blacklisted will know. The only way to get off a list is to be on a list of those people to be taken off the list.

How to... fill in a form

Forms are the lifeblood of bureaucracy. Every form has seven bureaucrats: one to write it, one to approve it, one to send it, one to count it, one to read it, one to check it and one to file it. The longest form currently in existence is the application to become a bureaucrat.

It's estimated that the average person fills out forms as many times in a lifetime as they make love. It's a small mercy that we don't have to fill out customer satisfaction forms after lovemaking or application forms beforehand (although this might count towards the impossible foreplay targets women set).

Some forms very helpfully give you a certain number of boxes in which to fill in your name. This is a subtle form of social sieving to weed out anybody with double-barrelled names. You'll notice there is never a continuation sheet for other names you might have.

Similarly, forms often require you to enter your full postal address on two lines. This means you often have to edit where you live so that your address begins to sound rather grand: The Larches, Newark. Often you make a big effort to squeeze your postcode in only to discover that the next line says 'Postcode'.

Most forms are very simple but there is always one little question that throws you. Your national insurance number, for example, is only recorded on a piece of paper that your mother keeps in an old chocolate box under her bed. Your wife's date of birth is similarly impossible to track down.

Some forms are quite famous. The P45, for example, is what everyone at work doesn't want to get as it means they're losing their job. Other lesser known forms are equally interesting. The P44 is what you get after doing something that very nearly got you fired. Best of all is the P1. In the tax office this is the form you fill out when you want to create a new form. In administrative terms the P1 is God.

Forms often want to know your age and give you a range of available slots such as 24–34 or 35–49. Going up a bracket is worse than turning thirty or forty because you suddenly realize that thirty-five is considered young old rather than old young. It's even more galling when they don't have a bracket for you at all because administratively you should be dead.

At the bottom of many forms there is a small box. This is the form's reproductive organ and if you fill it in you will soon hear the patter of many other forms through your letter box.

How to… fix things

Things are very like people in that at any given moment about one tenth of them are poorly. When people aren't working they go to the doctors. When things aren't working, people go to the fixing first-aid kit which is a tin full of old screws, washers, plastic hooks, fuses and odd pieces of wire. This tin has remained full for years because there's never anything useful in it.

There's a golden rule in life that if something isn't broken, you shouldn't try and fix it. An equally good rule is that if something is broken you shouldn't try and fix it either. That's what trained professionals with vans are for. In the past, fixing big things required lathes, blow torches and angle grinders. These days we have glue. Modern glues can fix load-bearing walls, rejoin severed limbs and keep children inseparable for months.

Things break for three reasons: you've used it too much, you've used it too little or you've used it like an idiot. In each case you can fix it by using it less, using it more, or stopping being an idiot. Things that need fixing then fall into three categories: not working, broken, completely buggered. Some men derive their entire self-respect from salvaging things that are completely buggered. Often they fix it so much that you come away with something totally different, for example they'll 'fix' your video and you'll end up with a go-kart.

Men are divided into two types of fixers. The first is the rusher and bodger who uses a lot of brute force and sellotape. The other studies the problem from all angles, selects exactly the right tool for the job, works coolly and calmly and tidies up after himself. Interestingly, this exactly reflects their respective bedroom techniques.

Most modern appliances are designed to give up the ghost the morning after the warranty has expired. At this stage you can either get your dishwasher fixed for the price of a new dishwasher, take out an extended warranty for the price of a new dishwasher or buy a new dishwasher for the price of a new dishwasher.

With mechanical things, a drop of oil usually cures any ailment and for electronic things a new battery will often suffice. Computers on the other hand are prone to total nervous breakdown, by the machine first, followed shortly by the owner. The helpline is the computer equivalent of your fixing tin: it's always there but is absolutely no help whatsoever. Remember, all computer problems can be fixed simply by turning the computer off and then going back to a pre-industrial lifestyle.

Health and Hygiene

How to... have a bath

Pouring the bath gives you a certain amount of quality time to do other things like shaving, getting undressed, folding the laundry or creosoting the shed. Bear in mind that if you take more than eight minutes your next job will be re-laying the floor in the bathroom. You should also be especially careful when pouring a strange bath. Other people's baths seem to be connected to some kind of major hydro-electric project and you only have to turn the taps on for the bath to be overflowing in seconds.

Baths should be hot enough so you can just about stand in them but you can't move your feet around. It should take a good half an hour before you can lower your extremities into the bath. Baths are too hot if you have to get out immediately with agonized whooping noises and then spend half an hour reading your magazine on the bath mat.

Bubble baths come in all sorts of stress relieving formulae which work by producing enough bubbles to cover all the bits of your body you're stressed about. Some people have big scrubbing brushes in the bath that they claim are invigorating (often these people use them to invigorate themselves without running the bath first). Generally, baths are for indulging yourself and you should make sure you have a magazine, tea, biscuits, radio and a selection of ducks within arm's reach. Also make sure the answering machine is on, you're totally up to date with all your friends, family and neighbours and the Jehovah's Witnesses have been cancelled.

When you get in the bath you immediately sink down into the hippo nostril-up position which unfortunately gets your hands too wet for reading. At this point you'll be glad dressing gowns are hung on the back of bathroom doors. Failing that, you can wave your hands about vigorously, run them through your hair and give them a final polish on the curtains. Finally, when they're bone dry, you can reach over for the magazine and then drop it in the bath.

Singing in the bath always sounds absolutely fantastic; you can reach notes well beyond your normal range. You can also reach neighbours normally beyond your normal range, so remember they may not be as keen as you on 'Bridge Over Troubled Water' first thing on a Saturday morning.

Drying after a bath is a specialized activity; women like to wrap themselves up like Cleopatra and pad at themselves whilst men like to saw vigorously at themselves (except for one area where they suddenly slow down and pad very gingerly).

How to… use a mirror

Before mirrors were invented everyone was as beautiful as they felt. Now the average person spends twenty minutes in front of a mirror every day; the more beautiful than average spend an hour a day and the plug ugly less than a minute. For some people, arriving at a mirror is like coming home and finally being with the person you love. Everything is a pleasure to look at and there are always new things to inspect and admire.

Playing with mirrors is an absorbing interactive pastime. If you have one of those bathroom cabinets with two opening doors you can look at yourself in profile. It's always a bit of a shock seeing the side of your head as it never seems to fit the front view of your head. If you then play with the mirrors you can get a tour of your head like a helicopter ride round the Statue of Liberty. This is not a good idea as it always leaves you with the impression that you are starring in a 'Before and After' shot for some product that gives you better hair, nose, ears, skin, chin, etc. Unless you're absolutely perfect, you tend to look like the sad specimen in the 'Before' shot.

Women are adept at using mirrors to apply make-up. They can use a mirror the size of a postage stamp to rebuild their entire face while standing in a crowded tube. What they don't realize is that when they've finished their face looks like the tube map.

Some mirrors are really friendly and make you look well-chiselled and intriguing. These are generally very badly lit mirrors in hotel washrooms. Others are painfully well lit and make you look as though you're waiting for the mortician to close your eyes and trim your nostril hair. When you're feeling low it's best to duck under these mirrors or clean your teeth in the dark.

Mirrors have an amazing capacity for changing your mood; for example you're at a dinner party being fantastically witty and entertaining and then you go into the bathroom and realize you have a piece of cabbage the size of a standard seed packet between your front teeth. You then understand why everyone has been laughing so hard for the last hour.

Of course a mirror image is actually the reverse of the real you. People looking at you see you the other way round and you can rest assured that you look a lot better the right way round. Trust me.

How to... clean your teeth

In the old days people used to clean their teeth using a sharpened stick. That was all very well when you only had one tooth and the bit you were attempting to remove was a shank of mutton. Nowadays we have a greater selection of teeth and tools to clean them with.

Toothbrushes now come with cleverly angled heads that allow you to reach parts of your mouth you wouldn't normally be able to reach if your fingers, hand and wrist were in a plaster cast. Moderate brushing up and down is fine but don't overdo it. Your gums are quite sensitive and if you brush too hard you'll push them back and end up looking like a sabre-toothed tiger.

Remember you only really need a blob of toothpaste equivalent to a small pea, not the whole pod. If you use too much toothpaste you'll end up looking like a rabid dog and be forced to spend at least half an hour spitting and rinsing before your mouth feels human again. On the other hand, if you suspect that you're an old compost breath, please feel free to use the whole tube.

Beware electric toothbrushes. The older models tend

to have the same engine as pneumatic drills and you have to brace yourself against the bathroom walls to stop yourself being shaken bodily into the shower cubicle.

Dental floss is the most efficient way of transferring small particles of food from the back of your mouth to the front of your mirror. In order to floss efficiently you need to be able to fit both hands completely inside your mouth with additional room for a vigorous sawing action. Americans love flossing and have, over the years, evolved huge mouths to cope with this.

The British are still a bit suspicious of people with perfect teeth. If you have them under forty you give the impression that you're about to sell something and if you have them over forty you give the impression that you've just bought something i.e. a new pair of teeth.

Cleaning your teeth is a pain but it's better than having bad breath, which is the closest most of us come to experiencing biological warfare. Trying to kiss someone with bad breath has a lot in common with trying to do mouth-to-mouth resuscitation on a very old dishcloth.

One of the major disadvantages of sleeping with someone on a regular basis is that you end up doing your teeth at exactly the same time. Then you find yourself turning the tap on and off five hundred times, head-butting each other and spitting great jollops of toothpaste on the back of each other's head. This often leads to a demand for separate bathrooms, separate bedrooms and finally separate lives. So think twice before brushing.

How to… wash

Washing is something we all do almost every day and yet there are no standard instructions on how or what we should do. No wonder the nation is in crisis.

First of all you have to decide what implement you are going to use. The most pernicious of these is the face flannel. This is an absorbent piece of cloth that captures all the grime, bacteria and pus from your face, marinates it on the side of the bath overnight, and then deposits it all back on your face first thing the next morning. Face flannels wouldn't be so bad if they stayed on your face, but they are also used on parts of your body that only your doctor or somebody who loved you a very great deal would ever go near.

People who wash in the bath have all sorts of washing aids including big scrubbing brushes to reach parts of their backs that nothing else can reach. But consider for a moment: if nothing can reach round there, how dirty is it likely to get?

Everyone agrees that soap is a good thing but no one quite knows what it's for. Soap can make you smell like a lemon which is great. But if you said you were going into the bathroom to make yourself smell like a lemon people would understandably think you were a little odd. (Pity the poor lemon plucked from a balmy grove to end up in your armpit. It's not much of a life.)

If you only wash one place this year, do your armpits. It's amazing how many travel, work and play situations require other people to get close to your armpit. Everyone will be better off if you get there first. You should also pay particular attention to your private areas. Genitals are the most badly designed bits of the human body with all sorts of completely unnecessary flaps, ridges and wrinkles. If these areas aren't washed regularly, huge fungi and edible mushrooms can grow overnight.

Parents have this thing about cleaning the parts of the body you never think about. For example, what is so important about the behind the ear region? Have you ever noticed somebody in public with filth behind the ears? Of course not.

There are a lot of specialist products for washing the face such as scrubs, exfoliators, etc. Be careful of these as they can actually scrub your entire face away leaving a smooth plate-like effect. Men wash by applying soap to their entire body, rubbing vigorously and then sand-papering any three-dimensional dirt off. Women think they will achieve the same cleaning effect by reading *OK*! magazine in a bath with a drop of ylang-ylang.

How to... shower

In every shared household there is one person who spends as much time in the shower as the rest of the household put together. If you're not one of those people it's almost impossible to imagine what these marathon showerers do in there. They must wash everything fifteen times at least to take that long.

Sometimes, when you've been waiting outside for well over an hour, you begin to suspect that there must be another door on the other side of the shower through which they disappear to another job or something.

It's important not to transfer your domestic shower habits to showers in public places like the swimming pool as, believe it or not, people don't really want to see you combing out your pubic hair, however neat a parting you end up with.

Women have something called a body scrub in the shower. This is a cream mixed with sand or ground rice or glass which removes the top layer of skin. This is a curious habit as women have just spent half their income on creams designed to improve the very same skin which they are now sandpapering off.

Men have one bottle of body lotion that combines as shampoo, soap and microphone for singing Frank Sinatra hits in the shower (all men sound like Frank Sinatra in the shower and all male hair comes out of the shower looking like Frank Sinatra).

It's impossible for a man to drop a bar of soap in the shower without immediately being transported to an unpleasant scene in *Midnight Express*. In order to stave off this calamity, many men opt for soap on the rope, although this in itself can often be a vehicle for other esoteric temptations.

It's an interesting fact that although there are many walk-in baths on offer, there are no lie-down showers on the market. Nor for that matter are there any stand-up-in baths, unless that is, your shower plug is completely blocked with hair and you have a very long shower.

An alarming number of people do things other than washing in the shower; if you burst into an occupied cubicle there's a good chance that you'll find the person inside shaving, washing their smalls or preparing vegetables.

The acid test of how seriously you wash in the shower is whether you do the bottom of your feet. This entails standing on one leg and propping yourself up against one wall. Make sure you don't prop yourself up against the door as this can lead to premature ejection and losing your place to the person who's been waiting outside for the last hour or so of your micro-washing.

How to... pee

What separates the male *Homo sapiens* from his animal brothers is the ability to direct his urine. This also separates him from the female *Homo sapiens* who has the same directional skills as the water buffalo.

Being able to direct one's pee doesn't mean that men direct it in useful or hygienic directions. That would be an unwarranted restriction of their free will and artistic expression. However, most men like to use this gift to do something constructive. For example, if a twig can be washed down a gutter, they're quite happy to do that service for the community.

When peeing at a urinal, a man will always find himself whistling a particular tune. Often this is one that he's not particularly fond of such as 'We're Walking in the Air'. This is because urinals all have their own particular resonance and will give you a note as soon as you start peeing.

Men like to pee against something, whether it's a wall or a tree. This stops passers-by viewing the offending item and also helps with a subconscious fear all men have that a small mammal will jump up from a grassy hummock in a feeding frenzy.

Snow-writing is a popular pastime in colder countries where a test of manhood is the ability to writes one's name and address including postcode in one pee. This explains why many Scandinavians opt for short names such as Knut.

The pee itself comprises two parts: the first is the main stream which goes straight as an arrow exactly where you want it to; the second is the final drip which has a mind of its own and can end up anywhere within a five-yard radius of its departure point.

From a young age boys are taught to shake, tug and squeeze this final drip out but, quite honestly, you could spend half an hour beating it against a wall and the final drip would still find its way onto the toilet seat.

Women often make a lot of fuss about men who leave the seat up. Real men actually prefer peeing with the seat down because this is more of a test of skill. In an ideal world there would only be a one-inch hole to pee through which would be a real challenge. We'd have to allow an extra half an hour to clean up but it would be well worth it.

In the average urinal there are two types of men: those who are taking the opportunity to have a pee before an event and those who forgot. You can tell the latter group because they are sighing with pleasure and whistling 'We're Walking in the Air'.

How to… be vain

Vanity is a big rosette for best in class awarded to oneself and worn prominently at all times. When you take a long hard look at yourself, love everything you see and can't wait to look again, that's vanity.

Vain people are generally very happy because they are in the throes of a passionate love affair with somebody who returns their affection totally and utterly. The good thing about being in love with yourself is that it's not difficult to be faithful. In fact, for a vain person, falling in love with someone else is almost an act of betrayal. Fortunately vain people don't tend to fall in love with other people; they end up wedded to people who share their own extremely high opinion of themselves.

Mirrors are where the vain make love. Normal people view mirrors the same way cars view the MOT, in that if you're roadworthy it's a bonus. Vain people look forward to half an hour in front of the mirror in the same way that other people look forward to half an hour of good telly. Their favourite mirror is the three-part one which, when arranged carefully, can give you a whole dance troupe of gorgeous yous.

To the terminally vain, the world is one big reflective surface and the whole day can be spent in self-worship in front of showroom windows, oven doors and chrome coffee machines. Some people wear glasses, some people don't. In between are vain people who take off their glasses. It must be very frustrating for these people in front of a mirror when they have to choose between seeing themselves in glasses or not seeing themselves without.

Vanity publishing is a cottage industry which publishes manuscripts from people who think they're writers but haven't yet convinced any commissioning editors. Early successes in this genre were the Bible and the Highway Code.

Old age hits the vain harder than other people. When you're the high point of evolution, it's difficult to accept that you might deteriorate and even die. Monuments are therefore very important to the vain in their bid for immortality. These range from an injection-moulded concrete lion on the front gate to an injection-moulded concrete smile on the front of your face.

Taking yourself too seriously is mental vanity. Academics are the worst for this which is why they often have the bitterest arguments over the smallest things. Lectures are mirrors for academics; instead of gazing at themselves, they get to hear the sound of their own voice which gives a similar warm feeling. Being able to laugh at yourself is the main guard against vanity. And you also look fantastic when you laugh.

How to… go to a barber's

Barbers' are the only places men can stare lovingly at themselves in the mirror without appearing vain. Sadly this often coincides with an image catastrophe thanks to the other man working quietly at the back of your head. Most barbers have photographs on the walls of models with classic cuts. You can choose one of these if you don't know what to have but bear in mind that these photos have been up since the shop opened in the mid-seventies.

The reading material in a barber's will be of two types: yesterday's *Daily Express* and a lad's magazine featuring the World's 500 Sexiest Women. Demand for the latter is heavy and it will be your turn for the chair before you've got past number 498.

When you're young you wonder why old men with receding hair bother going to the barber's. The answer is that they have more growing out of their ears and nose than you have growing out of your head. Similarly older men wonder why young men bother going to the barber's when they leave looking more idiotic than when they came in.

Barbers have three questions to get conversation going: 'Busy?', 'Holiday?' and 'Gel?'. It's up to you to turn these openers into a scintillating exchange. Remember you have a panel of men on the bench behind listening intently to every word you say, so stick to football, traffic and the weather. If you start talking about relationships, recipes or the arts, the next conversation in your seat will probably be, 'Wasn't that bloke a tosser?'.

Barbers do not recognize multi-part instructions. Short back and sides is about all they can cope with. If you want to feather the edges, bouffe up the front and highlight the back, you'd be better off in a salon where they serve wine and ask about your boyfriend.

When he's finished, the barber holds a mirror up behind you. This is the only chance in life you get to study the back of your head. For all you know it may always have looked like that and the barber's done absolutely nothing. Every barber has a sign up which says 'Tipping is not a town in China'. You can of course choose not give them a tip as long as you don't mind being hacked to pieces next time you visit.

Occasionally, a barber will ask you whether you want something for the weekend. By this he doesn't mean a bag of charcoal briquettes. He's actually referring to a packet of condoms and the implication is that you might be getting your end away that weekend. Before you splash out on a packet, just look in the mirror one more time and ask yourself whether there's really any chance of that haircut getting laid.

How to... take medicine

Medicines are a lot like media studies in that no one ever completes the course. Up and down the country people have little Museums of Medical History, otherwise known as bathroom cabinets. These contain pills and unguents so old that they are likely to kill rather than cure. The reason for this build-up is that all medicines come in two sizes. Two thirds of what you need, or a third more than you need.

Pills are the household gods of a post-industrial society. Every morning and night people worship at the shrine of various pots and blister packs to help them cope with the evil spirits of headaches, heartburn and wind. On average, people in this country take pills five times more frequently than they make love. Maybe they're taking the wrong sort of pill.

Some people find it impossible to swallow pills. They pop a couple in their mouth, drink fourteen gallons of water, and end up with two very wet, clean pills still in their mouth. Other people don't need any water to swallow pills and simply throw them in and swallow.

Often these pills get stuck halfway down resulting in a very healthy oesophagus. It can sometimes be very tricky to persuade young children to take their medicine. The solution is simply to smear the evil-tasting linctus on some delicious broccoli and pop it in.

Instinctively people believe that a medicine should be applied close to the illness. That's why it wouldn't feel right taking a suppository for a sore throat, or eye drops for piles (although, interestingly, suppositories can make your eyes water). Patches are an excellent way of taking medicine, although in an ideal world nicotine and hormone patches would carry the same kind of health warnings as cigarette packets such as 'Liable to be cranky' or 'Off my chump'.

Suppositories are a national sport in France, a kind of internal *boules*. The insertion of a suppository is actually rather a difficult thing to do and replicates some of the trickier yoga moves. It's no coincidence that they never prescribe suppositories for lower back pain. Hypodermic needles come in one size: large. There is another size, which is extra large but people tend to faint as soon as they see this one and can't remember much about it afterwards.

Placebos are very effective in medicine. This is something that looks like a pill but doesn't actually do anything. Even more interesting is the fact that over half of doctors are placebo doctors in that they have no medical training but just nod and prescribe a placebo. Interestingly, their clear-up rate is as good as real doctors.

How to... cry

The British aren't given much to crying. They used to cry on two specific occasions only; women cried when a loved one died in the war and men cried when they walked groin first into the handles of a lawnmower. In the old days, if someone started to cry for whatever reason, you immediately gave them your handkerchief. Often the state of these handkerchiefs was enough to replace crying with shock and sometimes anger.

Crying doesn't usually happen by itself and usually requires some kind of trigger like shouting. When you get really angry, your emotions well up faster than you can shout and all the words come out in big blocks or blubs.

As you start crying the immediate impulse is to try and stop yourself, especially if you've been brought up by parents who encouraged you to stop making that dreadful noise. Once you manage to stop, be very careful because a rogue sob is often still lurking under the surface and can re-emerge at the slightest provocation, such as someone asking, 'Are you all right?'.

If you really manage to let go, it can be quite frightening just how quickly a cry can become a howl of anguish. Once you're in full howling mode, other possibilities suggest themselves, like gnashing your teeth, rending your clothing and beating your head against the wall. Within seconds you can go from mildly tearful to positively biblical in your sorrowing.

At this juncture, the behaviour of the surrounding people is an important factor. If they get into the spirit of it and start gnashing their teeth as well, you can start a national wave of mourning within minutes. On the other hand, if someone says rather brusquely, 'Put a sock in it,' you might decide that you are actually making rather a lot of noise over what was after all a pretty trivial parking incident.

Unemotional people are often surprised by the natural high you get after crying. Crying is a natural detox as being racked by sobbing is like being connected to one of those vibrating belts that relaxes stressed bits of the body.

The significance of crying changes throughout your life. When you're a baby, crying is just your way of making conversation and getting something to eat; kids cry because it always used to work when they were babies; teenagers cry because they are experiencing emotional suffering the like of which the world has never known; old people cry because there's no one left to wipe away their tears.

Crying is actually a very ugly noise. If crying was very

beautiful we could happily listen to babies crying all day and that wouldn't be good for the survival of the species. On the other hand, different species don't cry and they seem to survive. Perhaps they do better sulks than we do.

SHOPPING AND SPENDING

How to... shop

Going shopping is like going to heaven but without the wearisome spiritual aspect. In fact shopping is the closest many people come to a religious experience. In shops you can take time for reflection in a full-length mirror and then receive absolution in the form of branded goods.

Shops are the only places in society where people ask you whether you need help. They will then treat you like the attractive and interesting person you could become if only you would part with most of your cash.

Shopping is not the same as buying; women shop, men buy. Women can enjoy shopping without buying something. They can even go shopping, take stuff back and still have fun. Men go to the shops when they need something. They find this thing and then they buy it. If it's not right they don't take it back because this would imply some error of judgement on their part in the first place. Taking things back is a form of retreat and therefore totally unacceptable.

Women like to go shopping with friends. This means

you have someone to hold the size sixteen dress you'll be buying while you try on the size twelve you can hardly get over your head. Men only go shopping with other men if they're exploring the furthest limits of their sexuality.

The golden rule of shopping is that the posher the bag the better you will feel. A bag with little ropes instead of handles is almost worth buying on its own. Once you have about five bags you should put some of the bags in the other bags. Remember, rather than putting small into big, you should be putting cheap into expensive. If in doubt, make sure you end up carrying the rope handles.

On the other hand, bargains can also be an exciting part of shopping. Women enjoy bargain hunting and will often complete a shopping trip claiming to have saved more money than they've spent. It's best for men not to ask to see this saved money. You will have enough to worry about feigning excitement/interest/approval for the mountain of rubbish that's been dragged out of the city centre without getting involved in economic arguments.

Men and women should never shop together. If by some accident they find themselves together in a shopping situation, the correct position for the man is standing just outside the door of the shop watching other women shopping. The woman then positions herself right at the back of the shop in order to summon the man in to look at something she has no intention of buying. This is repeated in every shop on the High Street except the one with interesting gadgets for men.

How to... shop by catalogue

A catalogue is basically a glossy magazine without all the tiresome news and features. It's estimated that two thirds of the vans on the nation's roads are delivering catalogue shopping. The other third are taking the shopping back.

Never, ever buy furniture from a catalogue as it has a nasty habit of shrinking in transit. The giant oak-carved banqueting chest that you were thinking of storing five tons of junk in actually looks more like a jewellery box in real life. The only exception to this rule is doll's house furniture which swells in transit so you can't get it up the stairs of your doll's house.

It's also worth remembering that the models featured in catalogues are as out of proportion as the furniture. In order to make the clothes look good they have to find models sporting vital statistics common only in the heron population.

However unique you think you are as a person, with an eccentric individual style, there is always a catalogue perfect for you. The way this works is they track very closely what you buy from one catalogue and then send you another packed with similar things until you end up with a catalogue completely dedicated to stone rabbits or white sheets or whatever bizarre peccadillo you have.

It's an important rule never to read a catalogue within arm's reach of your phone and credit card. The proper place to read catalogues is in the bath because the act of getting out of the bath and vigorously drying yourself miraculously rids you of the urge to buy a leather-topped fire fender.

Alongside every picture in a catalogue is a description. This is written in a style which were you to meet it at a party would have you making your excuses and hiding behind the curtains. The traditional style is, 'Problem you didn't know you had, here's a solution you didn't know you needed.' This has generally been replaced by the new style, 'We found this lovely little thing in Norway and we knew you'd like it.'

Catalogues are divided into new things that look interesting and old things that don't. Remember those dull old things in the catalogue are still there because some idiot a lot like you keeps buying them.

All catalogues have a twenty-four-hour order hot line. For smaller catalogues this is actually Mrs Berriman who isn't really twenty-four hours and certainly isn't very hot between eleven in the evening and eight in the morning.

The great thing about catalogue shopping is you get parcels delivered to your door. This cuts out all the tiresome lifting and dragging of traditional shopping. Although you do of course have to do all this when you decide to return everything the day after because it wasn't quite the size you were expecting.

How to... buy shoes

Everyone has a pair of shoes that they feel supremely comfortable in. Sadly these are slippers so you can't go out in them. Instead you have to wear a pair of shoes. People still wear sensible lace-up shoes but these days they're called trainers.

Buying shoes is a man's way of finding out that he needs new socks. There is a certain breed of men who go into a shoe shop and comes out shortly afterwards wearing exactly the same shoes only newer. These men feel betrayed if there has been any kind of design progression since their last pair ten years ago. For the office executive there is a popular style of shoe called the Oxford. There's also the lesser known Cambridge which is slightly flatter and the Oxbridge which has extra support under the arch.

The fastening on men's shoes says a lot about you. Laces indicate a straightforward honest type with a certain basic level of manual dexterity. A golden buckle says you sell financial products or are in pantomime. Any Velcro fastening shows that image is not important to you as your feet are not usually visible under your computer.

Women fall in love with shoes at first sight and then buy them despite them being three sizes too small and there not being any conceivable occasion to wear them. A woman learns to be sensible about shoes at roughly the same time as she learns to be sensible about men. For many women this never happens.

In ancient Chinese culture women used to bind their feet to make them look small and attractive to men. Tottering around awkwardly was just about all these poor women could manage. Fortunately liberated modern women have put all this behind them and wear solid lace-ups with plenty of room at the toe.

Shoe fashion derives from two separate sources: from teenagers' trainers and from special shoes for very old people with poor feet. Oddly the latter very often become hugely popular with the former. Teenagers invest almost all their fashion sense into their shoes principally to draw attention away from their face. As you get older the fashion centre of gravity rises up through the body until it comes out at the hat in your eighties.

In some shoe shops they measure your feet in a little sliding scale thing. If they haven't got your size in stock, they'll push down really hard until you lose half a size. Once you've got the shoe on, you walk up and down the shop feeling like a complete idiot and not thinking about your feet at all. For most people this is the most exercise they will ever do in their trainers.

How to... shop at traditional butchers'

For anyone who's grown up with convenient out of town shopping at clean, friendly supermarkets, a trip to a local butcher's can be deeply intimidating. We all have memories of our grandmothers ploughing confidently through the sawdust and saying, 'Half a dozen shank end of briskets, please Wilf.' Thirty years later we don't know what a shank or a brisket or a dozen or a wilf are.

Nevertheless, there are occasions when we are forced to go into a traditional butcher's shop, because we had to deposit our partner's entire wardrobe in the charity shop next door or our car's been repossessed, and knowing how to order is vital.

You can't really start by careful window shopping: during the summer months all you'll see in the window is a little sign saying, 'Due to the heat all our meat is in the fridge'. (In the winter, butchers have a little sign in the fridge saying, 'Due to the cold all our meat is in the window'.) When the meat is on display it all looks bewilderingly similar and the most attractive items are those little green plastic watercress displays.

Often you'll be tempted to walk in and ask for some sausages, not just because you recognize them but because saying the word 'sausages' is the closest one person can come to having a snog. Beware, butchers are a bit nerdy about sausages and will give you a list of choices as long as a Bavarian wurst (which he can also order for you).

It's worth bearing in mind that there is generally no helpful and informative packaging to be read in butchers' shops and instead you have a helpful and informative butcher. For your own protection don't ask whether the liver has nuts in it. To save yourself real embarrassment, remember that traditional butchers aren't overly concerned with vegetarian options.

Some people make the mistake of asking the butcher to recommend something nice for the family; before you can say 'payday' he and his young assistant will have hauled up this huge slab of upside of silver top-end sirloin. This costs more per pound than the EU subsidy on an entire herd. Even if you get nervous at this stage and ask for enough for two people, the butcher will assume that the two people are built like him or are force-feeding themselves to look like him as soon as possible.

Either way you will leave with enough meat to celebrate Christmas in the orphanage and a financial problem which requires you to head straight back to the charity shop for next year's wardrobe.

How to... drive a trolley

There are two main types of trolley. The first is a beautifully smooth, well-oiled trolley that goes exactly where you point it and doesn't have someone else's plastic bag and shopping list in the bottom. You'll find this trolley in the manager's office where it is kept for the exclusive use of visiting dignitaries.

The other kind of trolley is your one with the permanent three-wheel drive and fatal attraction to anything on your left. Trolleys, like dogs, enjoy sniffing each other out which is why you spend a lot of time in the supermarket apologizing to other people as your trolley gets intimate with theirs.

When you drive to the supermarket, driving standards immediately deteriorate as soon as you enter the car park. This is to prepare you for the truly shocking driving standards inside the supermarket. It's chilling to think that some of the imbecilic fatheads doing dangerous harebrained manoeuvres with their trolleys have a driving licence and will shortly be back on the road doing the same kind of thing in their cars.

Once you've unloaded your shopping into the car you then have to get rid of the trolley. There's usually a great big puddle of uncollected trolleys sitting in the middle of the car park. Some people give their trolley a shove in that general direction. Other people feel the need to be a bit neater (for men there is a deep primal satisfaction slotting your trolley into the back of another one). Before you know it you're clearing up the entire car park and pushing a line of fifty trolleys back to the entrance.

Many trolleys have special little seats for children which sadly still leave them within arm's reach of shelves. A far better idea is to put them in the bottom of the trolley and wedge them in with a twelve-pack of orange juice. Some supermarkets have little plastic cars for the kids. These are very like Porsches in that they're great fun to drive but you only have enough space in the back for two items of shopping.

Sometimes, at peak shopping periods, there can be tremendous traffic jams of trolleys in the aisles, especially around the bread and the milk sections. The cause of these tailbacks is often someone who has a trolley without a wonky wheel and is driving in a dangerous straight line.

For some reason many trolleys end up in local canals. When they're fished out and cleaned up they work perfectly. Apart from the wonky wheel. In fact that's very probably the reason they ended up in the canal in the first place.

How to… check out

One of the most stressful places in modern life is the supermarket checkout. It's the closest we come to those fiendish toll roads on the continent where you have to drive up at speed, select a free booth and then fling your money at a grumpy tollmeister.

The first rule is to select the right checkout. There's always a free checkout up the other end but when you get there it'll be eight items or less. Old women who have forgotten virtually everything in life can still count up to eight and if you've got one extra item you'll be made to feel like you're committing the crime of the century.

The poor suffering women on the checkouts have been forced by the supermarkets to say hello to customers and they get a bonus if they make small talk. But what are they supposed to say? You're eating a lot of custard tart? From where they're sitting, customers are no more interesting than the tins they're scanning and a lot harder to handle.

What they will ask you is whether you have a loyalty card. They really hate it if you haven't, because if there's one thing they can't stand, it's disloyalty. If you really haven't got one, offer them something similar like a Kidney Donor Card. You'll also be asked if you want cashback. Psychologically this is very dangerous as you feel as though you've made a profit on your shopping. Reverse the tables by asking them whether they want foodback, and give them the chance to buy the stuff back you've just bought from them.

It's very interesting to see the way people lay down their goods on the belt. Some people build a little temple with everything stacked in together which collapses as soon as the belt moves. It's much more fun just to put one item on the far end of the belt and then watch it travel all the way down before you put the next item on. While it's travelling down the belt you can run along the till and bag the previous item. This is great fun until the supervisor is called.

It's important to use those little dividers between your shopping and the next person's shopping. If you want to create havoc, try putting your sausages close to somebody's lettuce. That divider will come down like an executioner's axe and you will be viewed as someone with dangerously anti-social tendencies. Especially if the sausages are your ninth item.

How to... bank

Bank robberies happen a lot more often than you think. The technical term for them is personal loans. Interestingly, the time taken to pay off a personal loan is generally slightly longer than the prison term for robbery although with a personal loan you have an attractive conservatory at the end of it all.

Banks stick to a very strict principle: if you really need money you can't have any, and if you don't need any, you can have plenty more. It's a kind of anti-socialism. Understandably, some people refuse to use banks and instead keep their money in a shoebox on top of the wardrobe. Other people just spend it on shoes.

There are two types of banking these days, online or inline. Inline is where you queue in a branch and have to wait around for ages before you can do anything useful with your account. Online is pretty much the same except you're at your computer. The only advantage of online banking is that there won't be someone in front of you handing in five tons of copper.

In the old days you used to squeeze through the front

door of your bank and you'd be up against a line of bars. Now everything is friendly and welcoming with colourful carpets and the only thing between you and your money is your credit blacklisting.

In most banks there are a couple of desks in the foyer. These are not for general queries as these can be handled by a brochure. They're not for personal discussions either as these should be done in a private meeting room. In fact these desks are where bank staff go when they need to do some work uninterrupted by customers.

Many banks have a window called a Bureau de Change. The person here can't help you with your normal business as they deal exclusively with foreign currency. They don't actually have any foreign currency either as they have to order this but they do have an attractive display of current exchange rates to keep you happy.

Cashiers, like shop assistants in the lingerie department, are trained not to react to the size of anything they deal with. If you are depositing 50p or £50 million you'll get exactly the same level of friendly personal service. If you call putting an envelope in a plastic slot friendly personal service.

Banks and libraries have a lot in common in that they both specialize in lending. Where they differ is if you forget to take a book back it just stays in your house. If you forget to pay a loan back, they take your house. Unless you sell your stash of library books very quickly.

How to… use a post office

If you've ever wondered about the exact location of the frontier of the state, it's the counter of your local post office. When politicians talk about rolling back the state they must mean reducing queues at the post office.

To reduce queues, main post offices snake people round in a little sheep run. This gives you a chance to have a good look at the other people queuing and decide whether their parcel is really worth sending. You then get called to a counter by a little voice which says 'Cashier number seven'. Millions of pounds were spent getting the exact tone of this voice right. It's a beautiful balance between excitement about being next without complacency in the face of the wait endured. They got 'Cashier number five' wrong which sounds ever so slightly grumpy.

In smaller post offices queuing can often be a problem because only three people fit inside the door. If you want to bend down for some self-seal envelopes you may actually be committing an act of gross indecency. To make matters worse there is a sign which tells you to respect others' privacy by standing back from the counter. To do this you'd actually have to stand in the road. Ironically the type on this notice is so small you have to get right up close to read it and on the way back you're bound to catch a neighbour applying for state incontinence benefit.

Standing at the counter is like visiting someone in prison. They're stuck behind a glass screen, paid a pittance and are required to do basic, menial work with little chance of early release. That's why you should do everything you can to be nice to them, short of kissing the glass.

In foreign countries banks occasionally fail and everyone pours in to try and get their money out. The British equivalent of this is pension day at the post office which is in effect a slow-motion riot.

Many post offices are struggling to survive and now have to provide all sorts of other services. Look closely at the notices pinned up by the counter and you'll see that 'Bikini-Area Waxing' and 'In-Law Exorcisms' are now available. You can also buy attractive saving stamps to pay for these services in instalments.

Of course, post offices still sell stamps. There are two types: proper ones with an attractive portrait of Her Majesty and big colourful ones commemorating National Floorboard Week. Most stamps are now self-adhesive which comes as a great relief to ardent monarchists who have always felt slightly uneasy about licking the back of Queen Elizabeth's head, however respectfully done.

How to… pay

Payment is to capitalism what sex is to evolution. They are both the vital moments of exchange and, interestingly, both are moments of extreme pleasure. With sex there is the moment of orgasm and with payment there is the moment you get your carrier bag.

When paying you can either give the exact money or give a big note. Fiddling around with change implies that you have scrimped and saved for your purchase. Giving a big note implies you've just been paid and are living it large. Some people always insist on giving a big note with some change so that they can get pound coins back. Newsagents hate people like this and will often remove the colour magazine from your paper just to stop you being so smug.

Shopkeepers hate change. It's heavy and dirty and an average newsagent will lift the equivalent of three tons of it every day. That's why they don't like getting your change and they don't like giving you their change. The only thing they like are tuppences because they never bother getting these from the bank. Lots of prices end in

99p but if you buy two of these items, they're stuffed.

You should always check your change while your hand is still out. Nine times out of ten you'll have the correct change but it's always worth spending a few minutes checking for 20ps from Guernsey which seem to be that island's largest export.

The difference between a debit card and a credit card is that a debit card spends money you haven't got now and a credit card spends money you haven't got later. The good thing about paying with a card is that you can pay to the exact penny and don't have to carry a pocket full of change around. The bad news is that you will never be able to park again.

The lighter money is, the more likely you are to spend it. In the old days a penny was the size of a baby's head and weighed as much as a small piano. It was not something you therefore frittered away on sweets. A credit card weighs less than an ice cream wafer and is correspondingly easy to waft about and spend thousands in minutes.

Barcodes are the DNA of non-living things. Instead of you and the shopkeeper happily reading the price together, your item is snatched from you, scanned and then you both look up at the little read-out on the till which says 'Water £1.80'. It would be better if these displays showed helpful messages such as 'Tiredness Can Kill, Take A Break'. You could then go to a coffee shop and have your muffin scanned.

How to... complain

There are two styles of complaining: the American style which is, 'Give me exactly what I want now or I'll sue your nuts off'; and the British style which is, 'Sorry, that was probably my fault, I'll be on my way.'

The British are both famously tolerant and famously violent which explains why we're also famously rubbish at complaining. We tolerate just about anything until the point of extreme violence without any in-between stage. In future, we'll probably go down the American road where we sue at the drop of a hat because there wasn't a clear safety warning that hats may drop.

The difficult part of complaining is to speak to the right person. The person who you normally deal with is the 'front-line person' – they're called front line because they face the enemy and receive incoming fire. That's why the average turnover of front-line staff is similar to the turnover of officers in the front line of the First World War.

Sadly this front-line person can't really help you unless the computer in front of them tells them exactly what to do. That's why you have about as much chance of getting an intelligent, personalized response from them as you would of getting McDonalds to whip up something special for you.

Generally it's best to try and speak to the supervisor but remember it's a whole different ball game with them. They're super polite but underneath you can hear them saying, 'I've got a brain, so don't get snot-nosed with me, dear.' Remember, if they don't give you satisfaction you can always ask to see their supervisor. Everyone's got a supervisor, so if you keep complaining and asking for supervisors, with a bit of luck you'll end up speaking directly to Prince Michael of Kent.

The good news is that responses to complaints are getting better. In the old days they used to be variations on 'Piss off you old trout.' Nowadays you can be put through to the Old Trout Careline. If you really raise a stink you might be sent a Miserable Old Trout Voucher which entitles you to money off your next purchase of a product that you never want to see again in your lifetime.

Saying 'I want my money back' sounds as forlorn as a bald man saying 'I want my hair back.' Once it's gone, it's gone and the chances of it reappearing in your bank account (or head) are similar to being hit by lightning at the moment of winning the national lottery. You're more likely to get a voucher. Vouchers are the toilet paper of customer service. They don't get rid of the problem, they just transfer it to a piece of paper.

Similarly, complaint forms are like administrative punch bags. Writing down a complaint generally makes it sound rather trivial. Unless you can make your complaint read like the basis of a tragic Russian novel, you end up feeling you're a bit of a whiner.

It's always good to remember the name of the person you're complaining to. 'I need an explanation, Gina' makes Gina think you are either a very senior manager, a friend of her parents or someone who knows where she lives. That or you're noting down what her name is so that you can get her completely and utterly fired.

HEAD AND HEART

How to… worry

Roughly half of us spend half our waking moments worrying about things, which in itself is very worrying. Worriers are people obsessed with the future. They spend their time thinking about what might happen rather than what is happening. As the future never comes, their worries are never alleviated. Furthermore, the future is pullulating with possibilities, so the worrier always has a range of calamitous options to select for their undivided attention.

Worriers exhibit physical symptoms of their condition, normally a combination of permanently knitted brow, crushing headaches and fingernails chewed to the elbow. The reason they look so frazzled is that they are living two lives at once: one is the everyday one and the other is a parallel universe of unspeakable horror. Worriers are usually very imaginative people in that they can visualize in great detail how everything could go wrong. In effect they are daydreamers who specialize in nightmares.

Parents are forever worrying about their children.

That's because children don't worry about things such as putting their hands into food blenders. With teenagers it's slightly different in that whatever nightmare scenario you imagine they're involved in, it will probably be a pale and pleasant shadow of the truth. When parents stop worrying about the children, it's time for the children to start worrying about the parents.

Worriers are rather envious of people who don't worry because they think life is better for them. In reality bad things continually happen to non-worriers but they don't worry about them so they don't seem half so bad.

Some people specialize in worrying about the past; they'll wake up screaming about something they've done like spilling the milk. Worrying about the past is for advanced worriers as what you are worrying about has actually happened. In fact what these worriers are doing is worrying about the present and future consequences of a past action, so they get a three worries for the price of one bargain.

Worries come in several different sizes. Many people like their worries XXXL such as nuclear war, environmental meltdown or the entire disintegration of civilization. Others prefer worries in fun-size portions such as germs, unclaimed prize draws and unreliable egg timers. People prone to worrying often have accessories to help them with their affliction. Worry beads are one of these accessories, although research has shown that 7 per cent of what the worrier is worried about is losing their worry beads.

Worriers don't have the ability to keep still and let the universe wash over them. Instead they have the Canute gene which has them on the beach of life worrying that the tide might come in. Unless you live in Weston-super-Mare, it will, so relax.

How to… regret

People who say they regret nothing usually live to regret it. That's because when you're in the super cocky frame of mind that makes you believe you're well on top of life, fate puts a little set of invisible points in front of you and you go steaming off in the wrong direction.

Having no regrets means never having to say sorry. People with no regrets are emotional Pol Pots in that every day is Year Zero for them. Rather than having nothing to regret, they do the same regrettable things year in year out.

Regrets mark the little closed doors in life which we never got round to opening. Before you beat yourself up too much about not exploring any of those doors, it's worth remembering that many of them were actually all that stood between you and a room full of complete idiots.

All men regret not having kissed a particular girl when they had the opportunity. The opportunity may or may not have been real but the regret certainly is. That's why

Friends Reunited should properly be called Regrets Revisited.

Women also have long-term regrets, generally hanging in their wardrobe. This is the sickeningly expensive dress that has only been worn twice – once in the fitting room and once when you got home and suddenly realized you looked like an extra from an early episode of *Dallas*.

The good thing about regrets is that they generally have a limited shelf life. They only linger painfully until the overall pattern of your life becomes clear and you realize you had to turn down that job otherwise you wouldn't have met Brian who introduced you to hedge-laying in which you are now a world expert.

Regrets are little emotional hangovers. They have the power to make you feel bad long after the event has passed. There is also the sneaking worry that not only did you hurt someone at the time, but that their impression of you will forever be based on this nasty little thing you did. Avoid the temptation to phone them up and check. This will only give you something else to regret.

The teenage years are the breeding ground for regrets. This is where you stop doing all the good things your parents started. Ten years on you begin to rue giving up piano lessons, football training and formal education. That's why mature students' main study is mostly regret retrieval.

Interestingly, the smaller the regret the longer they

last. Remembering something you said to someone twenty years ago which was monumentally insensitive can still cause you to groan and cover your face in shame. No wonder you didn't get that kiss you were after.

How to... remember

Memories are the jumble sales of the mind. There might be one or two choice items in there, but most of it is useless bric-a-brac. For some reason the mind will remember things that have absolutely no reason to be remembered at all.

People remember their first snog, shoe size and where they were when Princess Diana died. People don't remember their own mobile phone number, their partner's car registration or where they were when Princess Margaret died. Men can't remember wedding anniversaries, women can't remember the line-up of Liverpool in 1982 and try to pretend this is less important than wedding anniversaries.

Smell often helps you remember things which is why men with no personality often wear a lot of aftershave in the hope that there will be at least one thing to remember after they've gone. The three favourite smells of men (of those that can be mentioned in polite company) are bonfires, tarmac and petrol. Mixing any of these smells can be especially memorable.

Beware of recovered memory syndrome. This is where your partner, in order to get the upper hand in an argument, completely makes up something you've said. The only way to deal with this is to deny you were there at all and insist that they were just imagining it. If things get really bad, say you don't remember who they are and ask what they're doing in your house.

Trying to remember things is difficult but there are many tricks to help you. These tricks are often very effective if you can remember how they work. Putting a knot in a handkerchief is one. Once you have four things to remember and every corner is taken, you can then put the handkerchief on your head. This will encourage you to do the four things as fast as possible.

Remembering people's names is very important because it can save you from social embarrassment. Let's say you meet someone called Paul. This sounds like pool so you can associate him with swimming. Every time you meet him you will think of a swimming pool and you can confidently call him Flipper.

As you get older your short-term memory slips but your long-term memory improves. That's because your brain is full and putting a new fact on the top simply means you lose the last fact you put in. The ones at the bottom of your brain stay exactly where they are.

For some reason people remember all the horrible things that happen to them and few of the nice things. This doesn't apply to sex where you cherish all the naughty things that have happened to you to help you during the times when there is very little naughtiness on offer (such as when you're single or married).

How to... be wise

Wisdom, like the household fly, is elusive. Unlike the household fly, you can't get hold of it by hanging up a sticky piece of paper.

However, there is a three-step path to wisdom. The first step is to watch where you step. The second is to put yourself in other people's shoes before you take any step. The third is not to goose step unless you are a goose.

Wisdom is the dawning realization that you actually know almost nothing and what you think you know will probably turn out to be wrong later. When you're thirty you look back and realize you knew nothing when you were twenty. When you're forty, you realize you knew nothing at thirty. This carries on until you're eighty when you finally realize that you actually knew everything important when you were ten and the rest was a wild goose chase (geese seem to be important in discussing wisdom).

The only people who know everything are teenagers. Teenagers know everything but wear foolish uncomfortable clothing. Grown-ups know virtually nothing but wear sensible warm clothing. Wisdom must therefore be the knowledge that warm and comfortable is better than cold and foolish.

If you were to read the bumper book of wisdom when you were very young, it wouldn't make any sense. You have to live through something to understand it properly. However, two people can live through the same experience and learn something completely different. Divorce is often the final exam in these shared learning experiences.

There is a saying that everything in life is sent to you in order for you to learn from it. It's not clear whether this applies to shopping catalogues you get in the post, but it's worth looking at them closely for hidden meaning. People who don't learn are condemned to repeat the same lesson over and over again. These people are called teachers.

Some people retreat from life in order to search for wisdom. The first thing hermits learn is a profound appreciation for steak and kidney pudding and a comfortable bed. But once they return to the world, no one wants to hear about that, so they have to concentrate on the few nuggets of wisdom they've picked up. That's why none of the sacred texts includes an appreciation of home cooking.

Wisdom is highly prized but no one quite understands why. You can't take it with you, you can't give it to anybody else and, in men, it leads inevitably to baldness and glasses. Ignorance, on the other hand, has a lot to recommend it as you can enjoy things spontaneously, like killing and cooking the Golden Goose.

How to... procrastinate

The guiding principle for every procrastinator is why put off something today when you can put it off tomorrow. Or this would have been a guiding principle had anyone got round to drawing up the guiding principles. Life today is so fast that people simply don't have time to procrastinate. Fortunately you can hire people to do this for you. They're called plumbers.

Procrastinators are actually very good at doing one thing almost immediately and that is to come up with excuses. As fast as you can think of something for them to do they can think of an excuse not to do it.

People who procrastinate aren't necessarily idlers. Some of them are actually very busy, they're just not busy doing the things you want them to do. Very few people put off doing things they really want to do unless they think this will get them more of what they want later. That's when procrastinators become strategists.

The big question is what do procrastinators do to fill the time they gain by not doing the things that need to be done. The answer is they are doing advanced procrastination to cope with the consequences of not doing other things earlier.

Of course, procrastinators think they'll have the last laugh because eventually we all die and all the urgent things to be done will lose their urgency. However, research has shown that procrastinators live on average thirty years longer than other people. In these last thirty years they have nothing to put off doing, so instead of procrastinating they're just waiting which is not so much fun.

It's very interesting to see what happens when two procrastinators meet (if they ever get round to it). One will be a worse procrastinator than the other which gives the latter a completely unwelcome air of business-like efficiency. Genuine procrastinators can't survive without the presence of an efficient busy person. There isn't much pleasure to be had putting off taking the rubbish out unless you know that there is someone close at hand desperate for you to take it out immediately.

All procrastinators live in hope that the thing they are putting off doing will develop so that doing nothing will gradually appear to be a wise and far-sighted decision on their part. Occasionally this does happen but then procrastinators don't get the credit because they invariably miss the moment to take it.

When it comes to sex, procrastinators are at a considerable advantage in that they like to take their time and not to rush things. The only drawback is that you may have to wait a year or two before they make the first move.

How to... be lonely

Loneliness is a form of social chicken pox in that people can tell you've got it and don't want to get too close in case they get it. Unfortunately, putting yourself in quarantine only makes loneliness a lot worse.

One way of combating loneliness is joining your local ramblers club. It won't stop you feeling lonely but after being caught on a ten-hour ramblethon with some of the nation's dullest people, being alone will suddenly seem a lot more attractive.

There's a difference between being lonely and being a loner. Being a loner is quite cool whereas being lonely is not. However, when you first hear that someone is a loner, there's always a slight suspicion that they wear a racoon-skin hat, hunt for their own food and have a woeful hygiene regime.

Loners are people who want to be alone. Lonely people are people who want to be with other people. Loners get lonely too but they just go further into the forest to sort themselves out. The loneliest people are those who are lonely in a crowd. They might seem to be having fun but underneath they're crying bitter tears. But that's what you get for supporting West Ham.

Being lonely with someone is worse than being lonely by yourself. When you're utterly alone you think that being with someone will be better. Then you spend time with someone and realize it isn't. And there you have marriage and divorce in a nutshell.

If you spend a lot of time alone, the world inside your head becomes more real than the world outside. When it gets really bad you have problems ordering fish and chips because you can't believe that a wish inside your head will result in fish and chips in your stomach. Very sad lonely people have no one to talk to and share experiences with. Very often this leads directly to a career giving illustrated talks to Women's Institutes.

Lonely people don't laugh. Partly this is because you don't need to show anybody you find something funny. It's also because you begin to worry that if you laugh too much you'll be sectioned. When you're at your very loneliest in the depths of the long dark night of the soul remember that the very opposite of what you're feeling now is an office karaoke night and be comforted by that thought.

Loneliness often goes hand in hand with feeling sorry for yourself. In fact the primary occupation of lonely people is feeling hugely sorry for themselves. Not surprisingly one of the quickest ways to combat loneliness is to start feeling more sorry for other people less fortunate than yourself, such as the West Ham Karaoke Ramblers Club.

How to... be yourself

One of the absolute essentials for leading a happy life is to be yourself. Annoyingly, no one ever tells you how to do this and there are no handy websites where you can download templates for being completely individual. Fortunately there are support groups for people trying to be themselves. These don't actually meet but there is a helpline manned twenty-four hours a day by an answering machine.

It's not always good to be yourself. The deeply unpleasant aggressive idiots that you sometimes meet in life are also being themselves. It would be hugely helpful if they could try hard to be someone else, preferably someone nicer and less prone to dropping litter.

Life starts without self-consciousness and other people are no more than badly designed versions of yourself. Then comes adolescence when you suddenly realize the first thirteen years of your life have been preparing you to be a total dork. For the next seventeen years what other people think of you is more important than what you think of yourself. This wears off when you realize that other people haven't been thinking about you at all.

Being yourself has fashion implications. Everyone has a favourite piece of clothing that they wear despite the deeply held wishes of someone close to them. People who are completely themselves have a look that no one else on the planet shares. Many people think they're expressing their individuality through their hairstyle. But when you look at photos of yourself thirty years later, you appear to be modelling classic cuts of the seventies.

If you're looking to be yourself, you should remember that you are what you eat. Sandwiches don't have to have cheese in them and a beetroot and mashed potato filling is absolutely fine. Just don't expect anybody to sit on the same bench while you're eating them.

Your sexuality is often an interesting manifestation of you as a person. That's why the best kind of sexual partners are two people who can both be themselves in bed together. However, if you're being yourself and the other person is bored, irritated or extremely angry this is not ideal.

In scientific terms it's technically impossible to be yourself. Sub-atomic particles change under observation and so do we. Depending on who or what we are interacting with we change to be something slightly different. We all have multiple personalities, we just buff up the one that works best at the time.

Only shy people are truly themselves because they

don't interact. It doesn't make sense to say you're a shy person underneath. Truly shy people don't have underneaths; they wear their underneath overneath without any kind of protective covering.

How to... exaggerate

Exaggeration is the salt of conversation. Without it most events, news and chit-chat would have very little flavour. Adding a pinch of exaggeration makes everything slightly more tasty. Sadly, we now know that salt is very bad for you and it's the same with exaggeration. Too much of it can cause heart disease, diabetes, strokes, impotence and death.

Most of us exaggerate about ourselves, what we've done and what we're good at. In a way we're all sexing up our own dossiers. Actually, not everyone does this. The only people who sex up their dossiers are people who think it's really important to have a sexed-up dossier.

Exaggeration is a lot like inflation in that it continually erodes the value and credibility of what you had in the first place. The normal process of exaggeration goes from dull but believable, through interesting and surprising, to amazing but preposterous.

Most of what you read in the newspapers is exaggeration. In fact it's surprising there isn't a newspaper called *The Exaggerator*. The truth is that life is generally pretty mundane but you wouldn't want to read a paper called *The Same Old Dull Stuff.*

Understatement is the nemesis of exaggeration. People who disdain exaggeration often go in for understatement on a scale that amounts to inverted exaggeration. Such a person would react to their entire house being blown up by saying that they were 'mildly irritated'. Interestingly, this works better than saying they were 'absolutely gutted' because understatement focuses attention back on the person whereas exaggeration can't compete with the big event itself. This explains why journalists are rubbish at natural disasters. It's difficult to exaggerate the effect of a hurricane.

All history (well most of it) is exaggeration. That's because any story that gets retold tends to have its dull bits dropped and its good bits highlighted. It's a miracle therefore when you get a story from ancient history that's a bit dull. For example, King Alfred burning the cakes isn't something you would even have told a neighbour had you been there at the time. But miraculously its dullness has survived generations of retelling without Alfred ever becoming the King Who Discovered the Golden Cake.

On the same note, all the characters from history who are titled 'the Magnificent' or 'the Great' were probably 'the Better than Average' at the time. In a thousand years' time children will probably be reading about Tony the Magnificent.

If you think exaggeration is something to die for and you couldn't live without it, spend some time with police officers. They talk in a way that is resistant to legal cross-examination and is entirely without exaggeration (almost).

How to… choose

Having too many choices leads to moral obesity. Money is choice in folding form and it's no coincidence that the rich are often unhappy. The people with most TV channels are also the people who say there's nothing on television.

Choice is a political matter. Are you the best person to choose for yourself or is someone else better qualified? A brain surgeon is probably best placed to choose how to operate on your brain but afterwards, you're still the best person to decide whether you want to marry the brain surgeon. Unless of course the surgery went badly wrong.

To make the right choice you need two things: perfect judgment and perfect information. The number of times you have both of those you can count on two hands and a foot. That's why most choices are actually a combination of ignorance and panic.

Hobson's choice is where you have to choose between two things that you're not happy about. The opposite of that would be where you had two ideal options to choose from. This never actually happens because it's impossible to have two ideal choices. Something's either ideal or it isn't. Unless they're twins.

Every choice you make operates at two levels. You can either choose something for the immediate result or for the long-term consequences. People often say yes to a marriage proposal because the immediate result is a wedding and forget the long-term consequence is a shared laundry basket.

Many departments of philosophy are warmed from heat generated by the interminable debate between free will and determinism. Let's just say that if you're determined to be free, you will be, and then encourage the philosophers to do something useful like technical drawing.

Anything that says it's the choice of a new generation has generally been chosen for them by the generation above. If you scrutinize the major choices that have moulded your life, most of them were made somewhere else by someone else. Repatriating your choices is the first step towards full adult life.

Life couldn't be lived if we had to makc choices about everything every minute. On the other hand, the quickest way to get a new life is to spend one day looking at everything you do and choosing to do it differently. But don't do this while driving or operating heavy machinery.

Making a choice means taking personal responsibility

for your actions and that can be a heavy burden. Often it's easier to blame your circumstances for your actions. Either way could be right. It's your choice.

How to... be fed up

Being fed up happens when you've had a lot of little incidents that are not bad enough to make you properly angry but have the cumulative effect of robbing you of your sense of humour.

There are many physical symptoms of being fed up. The first to arrive is the heavy sigh. These get louder and bigger until they mist up adjacent windows. Extreme fedupness is accompanied by aggressive muttering with a hint of the f-word.

One of the quickest ways of getting out of being fed up is to be well fed. This recovery process is called getting fed down. It is absolutely normal to be fed up at five o'clock in the afternoon shortly before eating. In bars they call this Happy Hour. At home it's known as Grumpy Hour.

A sudden overwhelming feeling of being taken for granted leads directly to being fed up. You'll know when someone feels taken for granted if they use any of the following phrases: 'Why should I?', 'Do it yourself', or 'I don't care'. It's their way of saying, 'I do all these things because I care and you don't even notice.' A small thank you is the nicotine patch for fedupness.

People who are fed up express it in different ways. At one end of the spectrum is the angry outburst when they announce that they are both sick and tired but actually seem to be remarkably healthy. At the other end is the big sulk, which is the emotional equivalent of working to rule. You don't give people the benefit of the doubt, the time of day or anything that could be mistaken for love and affection.

Some people are in a permanently fed-up state and become terminally grumpy. More dramatic is when normally nice people suddenly become fed up and release their inner cow. This is like standing on a dog's tail and seeing its teeth for the first time. It's a bit surprising because you didn't think something that cuddly could have teeth. A hug and a bun will normally do the trick in both cases.

Being fed up is not necessarily a bad thing because it's the state you have to be in before you change anything. People leave their job/partner/country not because they are happy but because they are fed up. So next time you get a bit fed up, view it as a positive thing. But don't get too positive otherwise you'll stop being fed up and you'll be back to square one.

Lying and Swearing

How to... lie

Lying is a key part of modern life and is vital for tax returns, marriage vows and all manner of sworn affidavits. Lies come in two kinds: lies that get you out of trouble and lies that get you into trouble. Often one lie can do both.

In poker there are little involuntary signs that give away what you're thinking; subtle little things that the experienced eye can pick up immediately like copious sweating, scratching or indiscriminate discharge of weaponry. Similarly, you're not a good liar if you do any of the follow after lying: uncontrollable giggling, thermonuclear blushing, tearful confessing.

Of course you never know who the really good liars are because they're never found out. Good lies are always anchored in a tiny particle of truth. For example, you're more likely to believe someone's climbed Everest if they've been to Nepal. If they've never left Huddersfield you're entitled to have your doubts.

They say that the eyes are the window of the soul. When someone can't look you in the eye, they may well be lying. Or they might have something wrong with their eyes. On the other hand, you don't want to make too much eye contact after a little fib. Staring into someone's eyes like a crazed bushbaby is also a dead giveaway.

Lies come in a wide range of colours: white lies are little untruths designed to avoid hurting other people's feelings; pink lies are things you make up for the sheer fun of it; red lies are used for filling in any kind of official paperwork; and purple lies are exaggeration taken to the point of complete and utter fiction, usually related to male performance in sport, fighting or bed.

Some people suffer from involuntary or pathological lying. Ask them where they are from and they'll say New Guinea even though you know they're born and bred in Huddersfield. Even when you start asking them difficult supplementary question like, 'What part of New Guinea?' they'll keep lying away with, 'Oh just a little fishing village, you wouldn't know it.' And then they'll make up a name which sounds suspiciously like a mispronounced suburb of Huddersfield.

When you think someone's lying, there are two ways of dealing with it. Saying 'I want to know every little detail' will force them to spin such an incredibly tangled web of deceit that they'll get irretrievably stuck in it and you can have hours of fun watching them struggle with ever more outlandish porkies. Or you can simply say, 'I've never heard such a pack of lies in all my life.' Best not to say this during the wedding service though.

How to... be paranoid

Not everyone is paranoid. Yet. Some people think there's a lot more paranoia around these days but they're mistaken. There's the same amount as there's always been but it's focusing on you.

For example, have you noticed recently that people always avoid you in the street and can't keep eye contact with you? What do they know that you don't? When double-glazing salesmen call they always happen to be in your area. Why are they always in your area? Why aren't they in someone else's area?

Another worrying sign is that however quiet you are there's always a background hum. This isn't random background noise, it's the noise of many people engaged in a giant conspiracy against you but trying to keep the noise down as they go about it.

Do you sometimes get a nagging suspicion that you've left a window open, the car unlocked and the gas on? You're right to be suspicious because there's a shadowy government agency dedicated to opening your windows, unlocking your car and relighting your gas when your back is turned. They also killed Princess Diana.

It's a worrying thought, but it's a dead certainty that your phone is currently being tapped. You can tell this because if you say nothing it suddenly goes all quiet. What about your phone number? Have you noticed that the letters spell out MIND CONTROL or WIND CONTROL if you live in the Taunton area. And have you ever wondered why you don't get any interesting post? It's because all the exciting ones from attractive strangers desperate to meet you are intercepted long before you get them.

In fact right now there's someone watching your comings and goings. They always take over the house opposite you and appear perfectly normal. The more normal they appear, the more worried you should be. The census didn't want to know how many rooms you have in your house – they know that kind of thing already. They wanted your DNA and now they've got it.

Have you noticed how the stars seem to be the same every night? Given the fact that there are a billion billion stars in the universe, getting the same ones every night is a bit of a coincidence, don't you think? No coincidence. They're spy satellites in geostationary orbit above your bathroom. So have your flannel ready.

Hidden messages are everywhere. If you look closely at the Bible your name, address and national insurance number are all in there together with the phrase 'death by sunbed' if you're lucky.

And isn't it funny how there was no foot-and-mouth disease in London where the government is. It all begins to make sense if only you're tuned in. There's a group opposed to this conspiracy that'll be contacting you shortly. They know who you are and they've got your address. Be vigilant.

How to... be irritated

Irritants are a form of life-rage served in fun-size portions. Often the most irritating things are only irritating because they're habits. For example, you wouldn't mind if people did that little flicky movement with their hair once. It's just that they do it five thousand times every time they speak to you and they don't even realize they're doing it.

However, pointing out something that irritates you is always a difficult and dangerous thing to do especially when the person knows exactly what they're doing, likes doing it and is not going to stop doing it. This means that whenever they rub their feet together in front of the TV destroying their slippers in the process, you're going to be irritated that they're doing it, they're going to be irritated that you're irritated and you're going to be doubly irritated that they don't care that you're irritated.

The biggest irritations come from the smallest things. Divorce cases often cite mental cruelty as grounds for separation but what this generally boils down to is a host of small things such as leaving the milk out overnight, intrusive positioning of elbow in bed and wagging of finger in conversation. Some irritants are so small that it seems churlish to mention them. Many a ruby wedding anniversary has been slightly spoiled by Cyril admitting that he's found Violet's way with a fork irritating since the 1920s.

Irritants aren't irritating per se. For instance, one day you can like someone a very great deal and find them congenial in every respect. A year later, when you've decided you don't like them, you find everything they say, wear and do intensely irritating. Familiarity breeds irritation in thc same way that armpits breed bacteria. For example, you have to know someone pretty well before you can start finding their habitual towel dropping on the floor irritating. A complete absence of irritants isn't love, it's a coma.

Irritation is a rather handy emotion when there aren't any really big things to hate. That's why you can find nice people irritating without any real excuse for disliking them. It is, of course, possible to irritate yourself. You can acquire things that you hate about yourself, little verbal tics like saying, 'Howdedoody!' when you answer the phone. That one can sicken you almost to the point of insanity.

Some people have a face that's naturally irritating so they're already on a bit of a sticky wicket the moment you set eyes on them. Likewise having an irritating voice, hair or general manner can be injurious to smooth social interaction. But remember that one person's irritation is another person's stimulant. You may find Dave winking at the end of every sentence fantastically annoying but Dave's wife married him for it. His first wife that is.

How to… be boring

Teenagers only recognize two possible states of being: you can either be cool or you can be boring. Being boring is never cool and being cool is never boring. You just have to be very aware that what is cool one day is boring the next. Unless you are a parent, of course, and then you are permanently boring. Cool parents are particularly boring.

Adult bores are divided into those who know they're boring and those who don't. At a party you might accidentally sit down next to someone and they'll announce cheerily, 'You've come to be bored rigid by me, haven't you.' For some bizarre reason it's impossible to leave after that. Instead you feel a huge need to prove that no one can be that boring. Eventually you realize that someone can indeed be that boring and you've been sitting next to them for three hours. When you finally manage to drag yourself away, they'll say cheerily, 'I told you I was boring.'

Other bores think they're very interesting because they're very interested in something. Unless they're in a club specifically devoted to Fans of the Stamps of the Falkland Islands, what interests them will be coma inducing to others. With these people it's imperative to avoid them getting started on their subject. This is harder than it sounds because they are always thinking about it and will seize any opportunity to bring it up: i.e. 'Did you know your head is the same shape as the West Falkland island?'.

There is another class of boring person who talks passionately about nothing. In an odd way they are fascinating because they are a living record of the unnoticed minutiae of life. For example, they will tell you in great detail that they went to the shops but they'll do it with all the passion and excitement of the mechanical voice in a lift. It wouldn't be at all surprising if that voice in the lift wasn't in fact a very boring individual sitting behind a panel describing endlessly what floor you're on and actually thinking he was being very entertaining with it.

Boring people are actually surprisingly dangerous. For example, the standard monotone drone is hardly noticeable for a few seconds but can, after an hour or two's continuous exposure, drill easily through the thickest part of your skull and destroy the entire contents.

One of the most chilling things in life is the realization that you are a bore. It's like catching yourself admiring beige zip-up cardigans. Perhaps it's reassuring to know that being boring, like wearing beige zip-up cardigans, is absolutely fine as long as you stay at home and don't go out and inflict it on other people.

How to... annoy yourself

However irritating other people are, no one has the power to annoy you faster or more intensely than yourself. Annoying yourself comes from a temporary loss of self-control when you do something that you know is foolish, dangerous or will have other unpleasant consequences. For example, you can have a momentary lapse in self-discipline and move your whole family to Swindon.

When you're going to a party you put on an outfit you know looks rubbish. You check in the mirror and the mirror says it's rubbish. You check with your partner who says it's wonderful so you know it's rubbish but you still go out in it. You spend the whole night looking and feeling rubbish and no amount of alcohol will quench the fires of self-annoyance.

You can also annoy yourself by deciding not to answer the phone during dinner, picking it up as soon as it rings and then getting locked into the world's longest conversation while your cauliflower cheese turns to cold muck two feet away.

It's frighteningly easy to annoy yourself in a restaurant. You know what you really like but you insist on having something else just to be different. Then you spend the evening watching your partner wolf down your favourite while you nudge a beetroot cake round your plate. You can also annoy yourself at home when you cross the thin dividing line between the second slice of chocolate cake which makes you feel richly satisfied and the third slice which makes you feel profoundly sick.

In the supermarket you can really upset yourself by deliberately and carefully managing to choose the longest, slowest queue. This, of course, is as nothing compared to when they've scanned in four hundred tons of shopping and you realize your purse is on the side at home. Or when you get to the car and realize you've forgotten the one crucial item you came for in the first place.

Most people try to stop unnecessary bitching about other people some time in their mid-twenties. But then just occasionally you say something fantastically witty and cutting which you're terribly pleased with until you realize that it will get back to them quicker than a twang on their knicker elastic.

Everybody has something that gives them a quick fill-up of self-loathing. Watching gardening programmes for the sexual content is a prime example. Or playing a computer game for twelve hours continuously during which you miss the arrival of your first-born is another.

People who say they haven't regretted anything in life either have massive self-discipline and never get anything wrong, or are massively self-satisfied and think they never get anything wrong. They may not annoy themselves but they sure as hell annoy other people.

How to... be bitter and twisted

Being bitter and twisted about something consumes as much energy as leaving a television on standby continuously. For some people it is a full-time occupation and they spend their entire lives re-ordering the world and everyone in it to confirm just how right they are to be bitter and twisted.

People become bitter and twisted for many different reasons. Generally something has happened to them at some stage which they think was unfair. They have been cheated, diddled, passed over, slighted, ignored, left out or generally not been given what they think they deserved. It's therefore a vital precursor to being bitter and twisted that you're the kind of person who believes they are naturally entitled to a very good deal from life.

Bitter people aren't glass half full or glass half empty people. To their minds, some malicious bastard has drunk the other half of their glass. Often bitter and twistedness arises when people have done very well for themselves for some years and then things go wrong. They forget that in life, just as in the stock market, past results are no guarantee of future performance. They begin to believe that the glittering prizes are theirs by divine right. And when these don't materialize the bitterness sets in.

Internal bitterness always shows up in some kind of physical symptom. This starts with a pinched mouth where the smiling muscles have withered away and moves on to the whole posture which is hunched against the blows of imaginary injustices. Then the internal organs start pickling themselves in acid and it's curtains to health and happiness.

Bitterness, like best bitter, ferments. The longer you keep it, the stronger it gets. Eventually you end up with something with a nasty green head on it that will poison you and all your friends. Interestingly, bitterness is a powerful natural preservative. Bitter people will preserve and even burnish a fragment of conversation or a trivial event from the ancient past that caused them grief. In their own way, they are little mobile repositories of long-forgotten history.

Untwisting a bitter person is an extremely difficult business. You could sit them down, point out that they're becoming all bent out of shape as a human being, and that it's high time they lightened up. Normally they will take grave offence at this and you will have given them one more thing to twist into bitterness.

The only way to save bitter and twisted people is to have a good laugh about whatever it is that's gnawing at their vitals. Sadly, if they had a sense of humour, they wouldn't have got things so badly out of proportion in the first place.

How to… upset people

Being upset is a flesh wound in the emotional battles of life. Upset people are walking wounded and will often carry around a small splinter of upsetness lodged deep inside them for the rest of their lives. Only immediate emotional attention directly after the upset will prevent the wound from festering.

However, it can sometimes be very difficult to spot when someone is upset. Often all you notice is a slight reddening of the cheeks and a difficulty on their part maintaining eye contact. The best thing to do is to ask them immediately, 'Have I upset you?'. Ironically, if the answer is 'No' you've definitely upset them and if it's 'Yes' you probably haven't.

Once someone is upset, getting them reset is extremely difficult. You have to find out what upset them in the first place. You may think it was because you went round to their house and told them they were a vindictive old badger. In fact they didn't mind being called an old badger at all, they got upset because you didn't take your shoes off when you came in.

What you did was accidentally wander into their own personal minefield. Of course some people's minefields are bigger than others and you can't breathe in their presence without setting off a massive chain of upset and offence. Often these people like getting upset not because they enjoy the upset itself, but because they like the corresponding grovelling, apologizing and furious back-pedalling it sets off in other people.

Normal people learn very quickly to tip-toe round easily upset people. This is counterproductive as they then become even more sensitive and easily upset to get a reaction. Instead, it's best to out-upset them. Anger always trumps being upset and a simple but loud, 'How dare you get upset with me!' usually flushes out any embryonic huffs.

Everyone has something deeply insensitive they've said or done in the past which still deeply pains and embarrasses them. It's the sort of thing that makes you groan out loud when you think about it. Oddly enough if you ever pluck up the courage to talk to the victim of the situation, they generally don't remember anything about it. In fact you've probably reminded them of it for the first time since it happened. They may then take the opportunity of telling you some other little things you did and said which really did upset them.

Facts of life are a prime cause of upsetting people. You may think it is a simple undisputed fact that someone is short, bald or big-eared and that passing comment on it would be as uncontentious as talking about the weather. It isn't and you should assume everyone is tall, hairy and flush-eared until they specifically tell you otherwise.

How to... be smug

People who are smug suffer from a superiority complex. Smugness is the conviction that you're just a little bit better than other people. This would be arrogance if it wasn't also mixed with a pinch of humility. Smug people know they're better and the fact that they're also humble about it makes them even better still. No wonder they've got that annoying little smile.

Smug people have a way of looking down on you even when they're considerably shorter. Certain clothes are an outward and visible sign of an inward and invisible smugness. For example, polo-neck jumpers are virtually the uniform of the smug. It's a way of saying to people, 'I'm rather cosy.'

The word smug is basically an elision of smiling and snug. It's beautifully onomatopoeic as opposed to onomatopoeic itself which of course isn't. But you do feel smug when you've said onomatopoeic so maybe there's some reciprocal justice there.

Lots of things lead to smugness. Having a house

which has gained more value than your annual salary gives you big smug points. A famous child allows you to retire in an absolute fog of smugness. Generally being well-insured against everything allows smugness to break out even at moments of extreme crisis, especially for other people.

You don't have to be rich to be smug but it does allow you to communicate your superiority in more obvious ways. Smug rich people are the proverbial Joneses up with whom insecure people think they must keep. Moral superiority also makes for industrial strength smugness. It's a way of saying that you already have reserved seating for the next life, probably quite close to the front.

In company, smug people always give the impression that they're hugging themselves or giving themselves a little squeeze in a pleasurable area. It's a lovely irony that the smug are notoriously rubbish in bed. When your starting point is complete self-satisfaction, there's not much motivation for further satisfying yourself or anyone else for that matter.

Smugness, like ragwort, is incredibly difficult to get rid of once it has taken root. The hot bath of achievement may have long disappeared down the plug hole of life but the scum line of smugness will last until it's scoured off by the brillo of ridicule.

In conversation smugness comes out in two ways: you can be rather patronizing about other people to highlight how comfortable you are; or you can be incredibly solicitous of other people, which is a subtle way of highlighting how uncomfortable they are.

How to… swear

Swearing is how humans bark. It's a way of showing other people that you're hurt, frightened or angry. Men normally swear more than women possibly because they get more hurt, frightened and angry. Or possibly because they're just a load of f****** a*******s.

Swearwords can be categorized into various levels of badness. Really bad Grade One swearwords all have a 'k' sound, at the front, in the middle or at the back. The exception to this is 'knickers' which despite having two 'k' sounds, you can just about get away with in polite company.

Grade Two swearwords end with a 't'. 'Prat', 'nit', 'twit' and 'twat' come in this category along with 'idiot'. Grade Three swearing often features unfashionable women's names with a slapstick addition such as 'flipping Nora' or 'sodding Ada'.

The Captain Haddock school of swearing combines unusual and expressive words such as 'billions of blistering barnacles'. These words generally start with an explosive letter such as 'b' or 'p' so you can physically let off steam with them.

Triptychs are very popular in swearing (in fact you can use 'triptych' as a swearword in the Haddock category). A fairly innocuous triptych would be 'great steaming idiot'. However, most follow the usual pattern of 'stupid' + Grade One + Grade One, with the middle word inevitably being the f-word.

British swearing tends to focus on the genitals. To call someone the vernacular of pudenda is just about the worst thing you can do (not literally – you could call your local vicar the 'vernacular of pudenda' and they'd probably think they'd been promoted).

However, in Latin countries swearing concentrates on mothers, whores and illegitimacy. Slavs bring animals into swearing, noticeably goats and bulls. Only animals with sexual connotations get harnessed to swearing. You don't cut much ice calling someone a coypu.

The unique contribution of Anglo-Saxon to swearing is the emphasis on self-abuse, principally the Grade One 'w*****' or Grade Two 'tosser'. In the United States this has been developed into 'jerk' and 'jerk-off'. Beef jerky, however, is something you eat and doesn't carry much weight as abuse.

Some people swear all the time with every other word being the f-word. Often this is because if you removed all the f-words, the remaining sentences would be embarrassingly short. The f-word used to be terribly shocking but now is little more than a comma in conversation. It indicates to the listener that you're moving from one f****** topic to another f****** topic.

Occasionally the f-word recovers some of its former power when it is used by someone who has never been heard to use it before. For example, a couple dropped into the Queen's speech would probably get the nation's attention.

How to... be a vandal

Vandals are generally disaffected youth who have been bypassed by the Scouting movement. It goes without saying that there is no Scout badge for vandalism. Modern vandals generally lack ambition personally and professionally. The original Vandals sacked ancient Rome whereas modern ones feel pretty pleased with themselves if they sack a park bench.

The root cause of vandalism is a desire to change the status quo. Moving a 'For Sale' sign from the front of one house to the front of another is the vandal's way of reordering the universe more to his own liking. The one thing guaranteed to stimulate a vandal is a 'vandal-proof' structure. In a similar fashion anti-climb paint brings out everyone's inner mountaineer.

Acts of vandalism come in two forms: those that need planning permission and those that don't. Of the two it's the ones that get permission that do the lasting damage. Wanton vandalism as opposed to planned vandalism tends to concentrate on bus stops and phone booths. This is a subliminal message from vandals to say that they're going nowhere and that no one's listening to them.

Most vandalism is fuelled by alcohol and the sound of breaking glass is really only an extravagant way of saying 'Cheers!'. People who create things when they are under the influence are artists whereas people who destroy things when they are under the influence are vandals. Interestingly, society has now reached the point where the products of art and vandalism look remarkably similar.

A clean wall is the traditional canvas for vandals to express themselves. The reason youths hang around on street corners is often because they're brainstorming what should go on a wall. Once you've written 'Botley Boot Boys Kick to Kill', you're going to be judged on it for a very long time to come. The worst kind of civic vandalism is the mural. This always features children, animals and a rainbow and has a depressing effect on the entire neighbourhood.

Graffiti artists like to write their names on walls. This is slightly odd behaviour as it's the equivalent of leaving your calling card at the scene of a crime. Sometimes whole walls are covered with the most elaborate coloured graffiti and then someone comes and demolishes the wall in a planned redevelopment. This can be terribly upsetting for the people who put so much effort into the graffiti.

Vandalism isn't restricted to the drunk and disorderly. The polite equivalent of spray painting is annotating library books. 'Lost Cat' posters are the projectile vomiting of the law-abiding classes. And if you really want to make a neighbourhood impossible to live in, buy a second home there.

TRAVEL AND TOURISM

How to... be a tourist

Tourists are people who spend their life savings travelling many thousands of miles in order to stand directly in front of you when you are trying to get somewhere in a hurry.

When tourists arrive in a place you can spot them immediately because they are the people seeing the sights. Sights are defined as being places of great natural, historical or aesthetic interest to anyone who doesn't live within fifty miles of them. For example, the last Londoner to actually visit the Tower of London was beheaded there. Similarly, no one who lives in Edinburgh has ever completed more than 400 yards of the Royal Mile.

The one sight that tourists simply can't get enough of is their guidebook. By reading it very carefully they can get detailed information about all the things they're not actually looking at. That's why all major cities are divided into two parts: the bits that are in the guidebook and the bits that aren't. If you don't take a guidebook, you'll see a different city.

Young people backpacking are at one end of the tourist spectrum with coach parties of old people at the other. The difference between the two is that backpackers travel alone but congregate with other backpackers when they arrive somewhere; coach parties travel together but then disperse rapidly as soon as the coach doors open.

Interestingly, 99 per cent of tourists go to 1 per cent of places which means that the person you're most likely to see at a tourist destination is another tourist. The advantage of this is you don't have to meet the locals, endure their cooking or speak their language. As a reaction to this there is now an emerging trend for tourists to go off the beaten track and there are many specialist tour companies vigorously beating new tracks to get to those unbeaten tracks.

The most exciting thing about being a tourist is that you have spending money. When you arrive somewhere you are a one-person boost to the local economy. Before tourists leave home, they decide on how much spending money to take. That amount is precisely what gets spent (plus credit cards of course). If you come home with more money than you started then technically you're not a tourist at all but a business traveller.

Tourists generally go somewhere to look at something. You can therefore be a tourist without leaving home. Simply walk to the end of the street and then turn round. Pretend you have travelled thousands of miles to see your house and family and you'll be surprised at just how bizarre and unusual they appear. Remember, you don't need to take spending money for this exercise but a guidebook would make fascinating reading.

How to... take a photo

Photography is the vital barrier that comes between us and our holidays. It gives us something to do when we're there and something to talk about when we get back. Taking a photograph frees us from the burden of having to experience anything. This is especially useful at sites of great natural or architectural beauty as cameras have all sorts of filters, lenses and devices to make sure you're completely protected from any kind of direct aesthetic uplift.

To lessen the impact of these moments even further, it's best to get your friend Brian to stand directly in front of the thing of great beauty and smile. In this way you can go halfway round the world and come back with a fine collection of pictures of Brian. This is probably a good thing as the people you show the photos to are generally more interested in what Brian is wearing than the World Heritage site he's obscuring.

Photos of groups looking happy are always a favourite. Sadly, the quickest way of making a group look unhappy is by trying to take a spontaneous photo of it especially if you take half an hour reorganizing everyone, changing the film, etc. In these group photos it's vital that you have someone with his fingers raised behind someone else's head in an incredibly funny and original way; someone totally blocked by someone else so that only their hair shows; the back of a stranger's head at the next table; and someone with blazing red eyes. It's worth noting the people who always have red eyes in photos as this is one of the telltale signs of a visiting alien.

Cameras are idiot-proof these days except no one's found a way of keeping the idiot out of thc picture itself. Of course there are a handful of people who look thin, radiant and gorgeous in all pictures – the technical term is photogenital. At the other end of the spectrum you get the person who always looks like the photo has been taken using a special bad-hair, red-eye, squinting-doofer lens.

With modern cameras, a telephoto lens can make it look as though you're standing right next to a grizzly bear. The only way you can tell it's a telephoto shot is because you haven't got Brian stuck directly in front of the bear smiling like an idiot.

Another very useful innovation has been the disposable camera. These are cheap little cameras which you can use and then throw away without ever bothering to develop the twenty-four shots of Brian on his own and in a happy group. Top of the range digital cameras allow you to manipulate the image after you've taken it, so if you accidentally take a beautiful, well-composed, crystal clear shot of something wonderful you can always superimpose Brian later.

How to... sunbathe

Everyone loves the sun and everyone, including white supremacists, wouldn't mind looking just a little bit darker. If you're white to start off with, this means sunbathing. Sunbathing is a fine art which normally takes about three weeks to master. That's exactly one week more than 90 per cent of the nation has.

Men sunbathe in the same way they would cook a sausage: intense frying until they're burnt all over and look disgusting. For women sunbathing is about avoiding any kind of lines on your body such as strap marks. There are two ways to avoid these: either you bring seven different cuts of swimsuits on holiday which you then rotate to expose everything in turn. Or you don't bring any swimming costumes at all and just sit around stark naked. The danger with the second approach is you'll be mistaken for a German naturist which scores *nul points* on the beach-sexiness scale.

The favourite tanning technique amongst British women is the synchronized strap adjustment where you move your bikini slightly every time you finish a chapter of Maeve Binchy. One note of warning here: don't concentrate on your straps so much that you end up with a massive white Maeve Binchy mark on your body.

Positioning is vital for sunbathing. For a start you need to be in the sun so anywhere outside the UK is good. To get maximum exposure to the sun it's important to move your sunlounger at regular intervals. Remember to reconnect all your straps before you jump up to do this otherwise you'll get all the nearby men suddenly repositioning their sunloungers to get maximum exposure to you.

Suntanning is a lot easier now we've managed to get rid of that pesky ozone layer. This is great news because people are no longer getting that terrible pale look when they die early. Protection against the sun is actually very important and a good suncream is absolutely vital. Anything that is factor twenty or below is the equivalent of covering yourself with cooking fat. People with sensitive skin need at least factor forty-five or over. The thick layer of white gunk will protect you against all harmful rays as well as interesting members of the opposite sex with scanty swimwear.

A secret desire of many sunbathing women is to have a mysterious tanned stranger rub lotion into their body. This can lead straight back to your hotel room where you should be aware of two things: there is no sun in your hotel bedroom so you're losing vital tanning time and, when you finally get his trunks off, he'll have private parts that are still so white they'll positively glow in the dark.

How to... pack

If you want to get to know someone really quickly, get them to send you the suitcase they've just packed for their holiday. Open it up and you'll get a precise snapshot of their personality.

At one end of the spectrum you get neatly folded piles of expensive clothes in a lasagne of tissue paper packed into a rigid black suitcase. At the other you get an explosion of assorted crumpled grunge packed under the pressure of three housemates sitting on it.

Expert packers make sure that everything is beautifully folded before stacking it neatly into the case. For people who have never folded anything in their life this is a bit of a non-starter. For these people the holdall was invented which allows the effortless transfer of holiday packing direct from the laundry basket.

A good way of packing is to start with yourself naked and pretend that you're getting dressed. In this way you will systematically remember every article of clothing. The only drawback to this approach is if the taxi arrives half an hour early.

When couples pack for a holiday the man often enters the bedroom to find his partner's case beautifully and neatly packed. He wonders how she managed it until he opens his own suitcase and finds it 90 per cent packed with the rest of her packing. One of the reasons for this is even if women are going on a potholing expedition they pack as if there might be a cocktail party involved somewhere.

Male packing is very straightforward. For a two-week holiday you need six T-shirts, two pairs of pants (one for best) and a Swiss Army knife to do manly things like rewiring the apartment, skinning rabbits and calming restless natives.

Women pack on the basis that, unless it's physically bigger than the suitcase, it goes in the suitcase. When they've finished packing, the house looks like they're just moved out. Light packing will typically include seven novels, bandages, photos of loved ones, purse, mobile phone, make-up bag, women's private thingies, handbag, torch, spare tights, thirty-eight pairs of knickers, little black dress, sewing kit, laptop, thermos, little miniature handbag, lip salve, personal organizer, fifteen litres of mineral water, address book, fire extinguisher, tissues, seventeen pairs of shoes, safety pins, last five years' receipts, four hundred tops, yoghurt, safety nightie, naughty nightie, mints, hairbrush, light bulb, eight magazines, anvil, etc.

However much you pack it's almost impossible to

leave without forgetting something. Experienced travellers know that the things most often forgotten are camera, torch, adaptor, pills, glasses and teabags. Experienced travellers remember all these things but sometimes get a little bit cocky and forget something vital like their trousers.

How to... buy a souvenir

Shopping is an ingrained habit and when you're away on holiday it tends to focus on the souvenir. Hours of shopping time can be dedicated to bringing something back that will forever remind you of the happy carefree times you spent in a foreign supermarket.

The marvellous thing about souvenirs is that they're different all over the world – you can get camels from the Middle East, sombreros from Mexico and elephants from Thailand. The one thing they all have in common is that they're made in China.

When you take a holiday in the developed world the souvenirs tend to be things that we have at home but cheaper, for example CDs from America, cigarettes from France and Ford Focuses from Belgium. In fact with this kind of holidays we've cut out everything else and just focused on the shopping.

In the less developed world, the one thing that is very developed is their craft markets. You can't take a coach trip to any tourist site without finding yourself magnetically drawn into a craft hypermarket where there are serried ranks of hand-carved elephants as far as the eye can see and enough papyrus to wallpaper the Houses of Parliament.

Ideally souvenirs need to be small and unbreakable as airport baggage handlers object to tourists taking out their precious cultural artefacts and tend to give the bags a good pounding. However, there is always one person who decides that they simply must have the seven-foot hand-carved wooden giraffe. They then provide hours of pleasure to other tourists as they manhandle it through the airport and have to pay for an extra seat on the aircraft to get it back home.

As a general rule, the cheaper the souvenir the longer they survive. For example, a 5p Biro with 'Souvenir of Tintagel' will write continuously for fifty years and do untold damage to the Cornish tourist industry. Similarly a miniature model of the Eiffel Tower/Taj Mahal/ Statue of Liberty will live in the back of a desk drawer for one full adult life.

The tricky thing with souvenirs these days is that everyone has seen them all; every house in the country now has at least one straw donkey, a doll in traditional French dress, a plastic camel, a gaily painted plate, a tribal letter-opener and a bottle of unidentified foreign alcohol.

Instead of buying your friends something, why not just film your entire holiday on video and then invite them round for the evening to watch you enjoying yourself. There's a good chance that they'll enjoy themselves as much as you did and you can also serve up some of the unidentified alcohol they bought you from their last holiday. And you can always slip a plastic camel in their pocket on the way out.

How to... send a postcard

Postcards are receipts for holidays. They prove to other people how much you've spent, where you've gone and what cars were on the roads in that part of the world thirty years ago. There are normally three kinds of postcard available: view of your hotel, view from your hotel and view of local attraction. If postcards did what you really wanted them to do there would be view of hotel room, view of suntan, view of tasty waiter.

You have to make a choice between writing your postcards at the end of the holiday so that they arrive home a long time after you do, or writing them right at the beginning of the holiday so that they arrive home a long time after you do. The downside of postcards is that you have to write on the back of them. It's estimated that 9.3 per cent of every holiday is spent writing postcards. Bizarrely this is almost equivalent to how much time people spend in the office working.

The three vital elements to the standard postcard script are room, food and sickness in any order: Lovely room, dreadful food, Alison sick; Dreadful room, lovely

Alison, sick of food; Lovely food, Alison dreadful, sick in room. Never buy a long panoramic postcard for somebody you don't really like as this will require about five hours to write and you will have to say more to them on the back than you've ever said to them face to face.

Postcards should be written on the penultimate day of your holiday so that you have something to say but you're not wasting your final precious moments. Writing a postcard home is normally the first time you've actually written anything since your last holiday. You then discover you don't actually know how to write. Fortunately no one can read your writing and few people bother to read postcards, so you can generally get away with copying out the ingredients on your suncream bottle.

Men and women have a different approach to postcards. Women pack their address book, buy five hundred postcards and make a big effort to write something interesting to everyone they know. Men sign the card.

The downside of buying a postcard abroad is that you then have to buy stamps. Every shop abroad sells postcards but stamps are available only at the local Chamber of Commerce which is in the nearby town and open for one hour a day.

If you ever wonder where all your spending money goes on holiday, it's the stamps. As people very rarely see the stamps on their postcards, they don't realize that they have put the local equivalent of £50 on each one. No wonder it gets home so fast.

How to... explore

In the old days exploring used to be simple. You simply went somewhere incredibly remote where no one had ever been before. This often took thousands of local natives to get you and all your kit to these totally uninhabitable places.

Nowadays everyone has been everywhere so explorers have to work harder. One pole is not enough. You have to do two poles and preferably you have to do them unsupported (without a jockstrap or sports bra). Mountains have also got a lot easier. For example, Everest now has a Stannah stairlift most of the way up. One of the few challenges left is for explorers to do a desert, pole or jungle completely clean-shaven.

No explorer worth their salt comes home healthy. When you meet a polar explorer, you would feel pretty short-changed if they hadn't lost a few bits and pieces to frostbite. If you are an explorer yourself, it's worth remembering that blackened extremities are the high point of presentations to the Women's Institute.

Similarly, jungle exploration is incomplete without

having lost five pints of blood to an insect that made its home in your trousers. Ideally you should also be carried out of the jungle on a bamboo stretcher suffering from some kind of malarial swamp fever. The natives have a special rate for jungle evacuation. They've also got very effective herbal remedies that would have you back on your feet in no time but they don't want to spoil the fun for you and the Women's Institute.

To be an explorer it helps if you have a double-barrelled name. This gives the impression that you're posh and slightly mad. After a particularly gruesome trip you can also claim that you lost one of your names in the desert, had to eat it in the jungle, etc.

Explorers need kit, the fancier the better. Victorian explorers used to rush off into the jungle in their shorts and spats which was one of the main reasons they didn't come rushing back out of the jungle. The modern explorer has hi-tech clothing that, whatever the outside conditions, makes them feel that they're sitting in the local library.

Another vital accessory for the modern explorer is a rival. This is another double-barrelled bearded person who has done almost exactly the same as you and therefore needs to be continually rubbished and treated with utter contempt. If he's just done both poles and said hello to an Inuit, you can claim he didn't do it totally unsupported.

Of course there are compensations to being an

explorer. There are those special moments when you stand alone at the ends of the earth, gazing for the first time at a breathtaking sight, accompanied only by an eight-strong TV crew and a satellite uplink to your family, your friends and your chiropodist.

How to... be on the beach

The beach is a detention centre for holidaymakers. Many people choose to get away from it all by joining millions of other people crushed into a thirty-foot strip of sand which is as hot and crowded as an underground train in high summer.

When you get too hot on the beach there is always the option of rushing into the sea to cool off. This is more difficult than it sounds. Even if you could rush through the loud unpleasant family with a windbreak the size of the Berlin Wall, you'd be stopped by the bank of shingle. If there isn't any shingle you'll get the line of stinking seaweed. While picking your way through this, consider quickly that the Japanese eat this stuff, and then continue rushing into the sea.

Wildlife can also impede your progress to the sea. Shells are wildlife in a dead kind of way and it is an unwritten law of nature that the sharpest shells on earth live on beaches. Razor shells, for example, only exist where children paddle. Shells are beautiful but don't take them home. Like sand, they're completely useless in a domestic environment and it takes years to get them out of the house.

Portuguese-Men-of-War don't exist in Portugal. If there were any justice they would be called Cornish-Men-of-Slime-that-Sting because that's where they are, that's what they look like and that's what they do.

Once you've picked your way though that little lot the next obstacle is dog walkers. These are people who've got the whole of the country to walk their dog in and they choose to get between your towel and the sea. The reason for this is that dog walkers secretly love to see their dog pee on your child's sandcastle. Once you're in the sea the final danger is horses being ridden through the surf so that their owners can see how much of a splash their dung makes.

Statistics show that 48 per cent of people who go to the beach don't touch the sea, 37 per cent only paddle up to their knees, and a further 10 per cent go in up to their nipples but just jump around waving their arms and screaming every time a wave comes in. Only 5 per cent of people go all the way and 90 per cent of them hate every second.

On the other hand most people on the beach have a nice cup of tea, read the paper, have an ice cream and visit the shops to buy plastic beach stuff in netting bags. It's therefore a complete mystery why all the deckchairs face the sea which no one likes instead of the shops and car park where the real action is.

How to... use a passport

Not so long ago, British passports used to be big dark blue cardboard jobs and passing them to someone was like handing them the wine list. In the old days what the British passport said was let me into your country or the Royal Navy will shell the palace of your dictator. What the British passport says now is let me out of your country so that the RAF can shell the palace of your dictator.

The other good thing about the old-style passport was that you were unlikely to confuse them with anything else. There's nothing more embarrassing than trying to get into Turkey using your post office savings book.

If you really want to see what someone looks like before you go on a date with them, check out their passport photo. That's what they look like in real life. It's actually against the law to look attractive in your passport photo unless you have an Italian passport.

Modern bendy passports can be read by machine. Many of these machines are employed by US immigration and sit in booths where they are programmed to be unpleasant. In America it's estimated that well over half the population don't have passports. These people are called Mexicans.

People like to collect stamps in their passport. That's why it's a monumental swiz that you can fly to all corners of the EU and get nothing to prove you've been there other than an oversized Toblerone. Good passport stamps have a lot of foreign writing on and fancy squiggles. It's best not to get these translated as they generally say something like, 'More proof that the British are an ugly lot.'

Some immigration officials stamp your passport willy-nilly. You should refuse to enter their country until they can stamp neatly. If necessary call their superior and explain to them loudly what needs to happen. Some really sweet countries stick a little postage stamp in your passport. This covers some kind of government airport duty when you arrive in the country. In Britain we also have stamp duty but this is how our government punishes us for staying at home.

One person in every hundred forgets their passport when they go on holiday. Interestingly, one person in every hundred caught speeding is driving home to get their passport. Losing your passport when abroad is very, very tiresome. It means going to the consulate and interrupting their cocktails and, not surprisingly, you then get the Too Stupid To Have a Passport treatment.

On the upside, given the brisk trade in stolen passports, your own passport is likely to get home before you do, albeit with a slightly different photo.

How to... be security checked

Security checks are a cross between the police and your mother in that they're just a tougher way of saying you're not going through the door in that.

Obviously sharp objects are no longer acceptable when travelling and it's now hard to see how the Swiss army will ever fight abroad. If for some reason you forget that you're carrying a sharp object it will be confiscated from you. It's like being back at school except for the fact that the knives you carry are now a lot smaller.

People love having their bags searched. It's a mini-equivalent of starring in *Through the Keyhole* where you get to display your intimate personal things to complete strangers. Some people open their bags and the contents look as if they've already been thoroughly ransacked. Other people pack so neatly that just lifting the corner of one pair of underpants makes it virtually impossible to repack. Many husbands have never seen the inside of their wife's handbag and there can be quite a frisson seeing another man giving it a good once-over.

Metal detectors are technological confessionals. Experienced travellers know precisely, at any given moment, exactly what metal they have on their person. Theoretically this allows you to whistle through security checks. In practice the person in front of you has had a number of horrific car accidents and been rebuilt from the ground up with titanium spare parts. You then have to wait while he is deconstructed and various bits of him are passed through in a plastic tray.

The one thing you're not allowed to take through security is a sense of humour. Never make jokes during your frisking about having an anti-tank weapon concealed in a remote orifice. Security personnel are trained to find anti-tank weapons in remote orifices and will welcome the opportunity to practise their search-and-rescue techniques.

Occasionally, as part of the checking, you will be singled out for frisking. Remember, it is not necessary to undress for this procedure and put your clothing in the plastic tray. Simply stand as if you were about to do a star-jump. You will then be very briefly skimmed lightly all over. This whole procedure is based on the average male idea of foreplay.

The metal detector is the closest most people get to a truth detector and it's amazing what you can find out. For example, you can be going through with a friend when they suddenly remember that they've got a four-